ADVANCE PRAISE FOR

Mapping Holistic Learning

"This book fills a great need that has existed since our world of reading and writing became so multimodal. Boyd White and Amélie Lemieux provide an entrée into the world of aesthetics for any teacher who is interested in adding to their students' responsive palettes. The technique of using 'aesthetigrams,' as described by White and Lemieux, will enable teachers and students to share a common vocabulary for articulating what is often difficult to articulate."

> —*William Kist, Professor, Kent State University, Author,*
> New Literacies in Action and Getting Started with Blended Learning

"This book has at its core art and aesthetics. It is beautifully written prose about the use of aesthetigrams, and other arts-based and creative approaches, with both under and post-graduate students. The method and way of thinking with aesthetigrams allows students and researchers to visually map their individual interactions with art, aesthetics and philosophy. A theoretical, strong text, the book provides accessible and practical implications for the use of aesthetigrams across a range of contexts. Boyd, for example, shares his experiences teaching in higher education whereby students, who come from a range of personal, social and cultural backgrounds, are encouraged to utilise their own capabilities to perceive art and aesthetic experience. Through the use of aesthetigrams students reflect, ponder and 'feel/smell/taste' art. Later in the text, another example with a focus on poetry shows the powerful results of such reflective and reflexive approaches. Lemieux applies the method in a secondary school classroom context in relation to literature. Students are requested to respond to a literary play through ekphrastic writing as well as aesthetigrams. Students show deeper understandings of artistic works as a result of the methods outlined in this text. I would recommend other educators who work in similar areas to embrace this book. While the ultimate goal is for students to appreciate and critique art, what happens in reality is their own personal transformations in 'living,' 'engaging,' 'being in flow' and 'becoming wide-awake.'"

> —*Georgina Barton, Associate Professor of Literacies and Pedagogy,*
> *University of Southern Queensland*

"In this book readers can find some important clues and insights regarding ways to capture, share, and discuss the emotional and aesthetic reactions of young readers to texts of all types: written, visual, and auditory. Based on a solid grounding of phenomenological theory, the authors provide lots of examples and illustrations of ways to tackle one of the most persistent issues of teaching and learning. My favorite participant quote is from the second grade student who described the way his body feels like a volcano during philosophical enquiry! This is a feeling that we can relate to, and seek out in our classrooms. An original and highly recommended text."

> —*Ralf St. Clair, Dean of Education at Victoria University*

Mapping Holistic Learning

This book is part of the Peter Lang Education list.
Every volume is peer reviewed and meets
the highest quality standards for content and production.

PETER LANG
New York • Bern • Frankfurt • Berlin
Brussels • Vienna • Oxford • Warsaw

Boyd White and Amélie Lemieux

Mapping Holistic Learning

An Introductory Guide to Aesthetigrams

PETER LANG
New York • Bern • Frankfurt • Berlin
Brussels • Vienna • Oxford • Warsaw

Library of Congress Cataloging-in-Publication Data

Names: White, Boyd, author. | Lemieux, Amélie, author.
Title: Mapping holistic learning: an introductory guide to aesthetigrams /
Boyd White and Amélie Lemieux.
Description: New York: Peter Lang, 2017.
Includes bibliographical references and index.
Identifiers: LCCN 2017017080 | ISBN 978-1-4331-3277-3 (hardback)
ISBN 978-1-4331-3276-6 (pbk.: alk. paper) | ISBN 978-14331-4468-4 (ebook pdf)
ISBN 978-1-4331-4469-1 (epub) | ISBN 978-1-4331-4470-7 (mobi)
Subjects: LCSH: Holistic education. | Phenomenology and literature.
Aesthetics—Study and teaching.
Classification: LCC LC990 .W56 2017 | DDC 370.112—dc23
LC record available at https://lccn.loc.gov/2017017080
DOI 10.3726/b11285

Bibliographic information published by **Die Deutsche Nationalbibliothek.**
Die Deutsche Nationalbibliothek lists this publication in the "Deutsche
Nationalbibliografie"; detailed bibliographic data are available
on the Internet at http://dnb.d-nb.de/.

© 2017 Peter Lang Publishing, Inc., New York
29 Broadway, 18th floor, New York, NY 10006
www.peterlang.com

Table OF Contents

List OF Figures

Acknowledgements

First, the authors would like to thank Peter Lang Publishing for their support of this project.

For my part I also want to thank the many students and friends over the years who have helped develop and refine the aesthetigram strategy. Their questions and suggestions continue to inspire my learning and, I hope, my teaching.

—Boyd White

I am grateful that Boyd encouraged my pursuit of the aesthetigram idea in new directions, including the field of literacy. I am also thankful for the Social Sciences and Humanities Research Council of Canada's financial support to undertake research on adolescent boys' reading engagement through aesthetigram making.

—Amélie Lemieux

I would like to thank the youth board and facilitation team of Brila Youth Projects for their enthusiastic commitment to creating the first philosograms.

—Natalie Fletcher

Introduction

BOYD WHITE AND AMÉLIE LEMIEUX

This book relies heavily on research conducted over the past 2 years of fieldwork in the Greater Montreal area, both in university and secondary school settings, although the beginnings of that research stretch much further back, as the next section will describe. While our examples focus on visual art, literature, poetry, and philosophy for children, it is our hope that the book will inspire teachers across the curricular spectrum to consider ways to insert attention to aesthetic experience in their respective classes. But the book is not just for educators. We hope that anyone with an interest in expanding her or his aesthetic engagement, whether that be, for example, in interactions with artworks, or the writing of poetry, will find this book useful. We have divided the text into three sections. The first addresses the theoretical framework that underpins our research. The second, Chapters 2–5, provides examples of aesthetigram usage within the formal education environment, in art and literature classrooms. The third section introduces two recent experiments in informal settings, one in an adult poetry workshop, the other in a philosophy-for-children workshop. It is not necessary to follow the book in chronological order. We invite you to choose whatever seems most relevant to your interests.

A SHORT HISTORY OF AESTHETIGRAMS

The origins of this text began many years ago. I was teaching a pre-service teacher education course titled *Aesthetics and art criticism for the classroom* within the Faculty of Education at McGill University. Originally, I designed the course to augment the studio courses that our Department of Education in the Arts offered at that time. My rationale was that even our senior students, some of whom were quite accomplished studio practitioners, were often at a loss when it came to engaging in discussions about art. They were just beginning to find their identities as fledgling artists and tended to be somewhat dogmatic in their opinions. This, I felt, was not a good stance for engaging young students in classroom discussions about art, not if we wanted to encourage open-mindedness, a willingness to entertain others' perspectives, and acknowledge that there is no one single correct meaning to artworks (although it is possible to be wrong too).

And so I began the course. It consisted of readings by various educators who introduced differing strategies for entering into encounters with artworks and we tried these strategies out through classroom exercises and visits to museums and galleries. This was the aesthetics part of the course. That is, I was more intent on introducing the concept of aesthetic experience—what takes place within encounters with artworks—than on aesthetic theory per se. My orientation was functional as opposed to one with an emphasis on principles of, for example, beauty. Of course, inevitably discussion did emerge around definitions of art, the place (or not) or beauty in art and in life, the role of personal taste and judgement, whether Kant's notion of disinterest is helpful or a hindrance to engagements with art. These and many other philosophical questions did come up. But, as a teacher, what really interested me was the question of what was taking place in the minds of my students as they interacted with artworks. How could I engage my students in fruitful discussions about their experiences, and perhaps challenge them to further their explorations, if I didn't know what was going on within the private and fleeting world of their interactions? As well, I was interested in contributing to research, to ongoing discussions about definitions of aesthetic experience. I needed a pedagogical strategy. What I came up with is what I call aesthetigrams. These are participant-created visual maps that document an individual's interactions with artworks moment by moment. They provide a concrete record to which the student and I can refer to assist in our discussions about what took place. So they are an aid to teaching as well as a self-learning device. We will offer more details about how aesthetigrams work within differing contexts in the coming chapters.

The aesthetigrams were also my lead-in to art criticism. That is, to counter the tendency towards dogmatism that I mentioned above, for the latter part of the course I encouraged the writing of experientially oriented critiques, as opposed to ones that required the making of judgements about the worth of an artwork within the artworld pantheon. My students did not have the art history backgrounds to make those kinds of judgements. What they did have was an awareness of the significance of particular artworks to themselves personally.

And the aesthetigrams gave them a framework upon which to build their critiques. These became valuable sources of educational exchange, for shared learning.

Gradually undergraduate students from across the Education Faculty as well as other Faculties began to attend the course. Most had little or no background in art, but they did bring varied backgrounds and life experiences to the course. The mix of backgrounds became the norm. The Department of Education in the Arts ultimately was folded into another Department due to staff retirements and low registrations, but I continued to offer the course, and still do. It is always full. Generalist pre-service teachers take the course because, as potential elementary school teachers, they anticipate having to teach art; it is one of the requirements within the provincial curriculum. The Faculty still offers some basic studio courses. So students can acquire a degree of confidence in the handling of studio materials and techniques through these courses. The *Aesthetics and Art Criticism* course provides pre-service teachers with the confidence to engage their prospective students in talk about art through a better understanding of their own ways of making meaning, with the help of aesthetigrams. But art is not necessarily the end point. As students from other Faculties have indicated, an awareness of how aesthetic encounters enlarge one's engagement in the world at large has been an important part of their educational growth.

At the graduate-level I teach a parallel course, *Aesthetics and Education*. This course focuses more on educational theory, compared to the undergraduate one, which emphasizes classroom application. But I incorporate the aesthetigram strategy with the graduate students too in order that the learning is not limited to a grasp of theoretical concepts. Practice in the making of aesthetigrams enables students to check and challenge the theory by referring to records of their own personal experience. Their understanding of what it means to be aesthetically involved thus combines theory and practice.

Above I have described how the aesthetigram strategy emerged out of my university teaching. A premise of this text, however, is that aesthetic encounters have their place not only across the formal curriculum but in informal venues as well. In terms of formal education I hope, with this text, to spur a broader application of the aesthetigram strategy among educators across the curricular spectrum. With age-appropriate variations, I am persuaded that students from K–12 and post-secondary levels can be introduced to educationally valuable, aesthetically funded interactions in most, if not all, subject areas. Then too, our daily lives provide much of our learning. Often we absorb that learning non-reflectively. But sometimes it helps to reinforce that learning by understanding the patterns of our responses to those learning situations. Aesthetigrams may be useful here too. In later chapters, we will be describing a few examples of these varied contexts.

AESTHETIC EXPERIENCE

Above, I have used the terms aesthetic experience, aesthetic encounter, and aesthetic engagement interchangeably. The terms deserve a little elaboration. That is, what do I mean by these terms? At the risk of oversimplifying the topic, I would say that aesthetic experience is an act of perception, what the ancient Greeks termed *aisthetikos*, which means perception by the senses. But perception is not just mechanical, like a surveillance camera. Perception of the sort I am referring to requires visual, aural, olfactory, and/or somatic acuity, combined with, first, some form of affective response (not necessarily full-blown emotion). I will attribute these faculties to the body. Perceptions instigate a second step or state of awareness— a sense of connectedness—to previous related experiences (memory) or, in a metaphoric sense, to something larger. This latter awareness is what some might call a spiritual sense. Third, together these acts of awareness culminate in a sense of personal significance (mind). In other words, aesthetic experience involves the whole person—body, mind, and spirit. It is not the same for everyone; there is more than one kind of aesthetic experience. And the same stimulus may incite variable responses even in the same person. Further, there may be small experiences or life changing ones and everything in between. But from an educational perspective the significance of aesthetic experience is that it involves the whole person. I argue that at least part of the malaise in the enterprise of schooling may be traced to the tendency to address only one part of the person, usually the mind, to the exclusion of the body and/or one's affective state.

II

AMÉLIE'S PERSPECTIVE ON AESTHETIC ENCOUNTERS

The first class I took with Boyd White was *Philosophical Foundations of Education*, a required course for undergraduate students completing their Bachelor's in Education. Apart from providing familiarity with some of the most pivotal philosophical questions in education, the premise of this course was to make students think about reflective teaching practices. One of these practises was to be able to recognize one's own values, affinities, and biases through the lens of aesthetic experiences. That is, philosophy of education lends itself to the study of self in relation to the world, and we argue that this book provides guidelines to explore these matters in a variety of classes including, but not limited to, a philosophy class.

In this class, students were introduced to the concept of aesthetic experience through provoking questions regarding viewing experiences of a painting—Martha Teles' *The Gift*—and a photograph—Catherine Opie's *Self Portrait Nursing*. The artworks were projected on a white classroom screen in an auditorium filled with 80 students. Both art pieces were provocative in their own way, the first because it challenged depth perception and knowledge of conventional geometric figures, t he second as it depicted a short-haired, tattooed woman, breastfeeding her infant. White detailed the aesthetic reception of *The Gift* and *Self Portrait Nursing*, and the implications of aesthetic theory in art education in his 2011 article: Private Perceptions, Public Reflections: Aesthetic Encounters to Shared Meaning Making, *The International Journal of Education & the Arts*. I recall the discussions we had in class about the nature of these works, how our shared experiences morphed into a future interest in the research that I am doing today towards intersubjectivity and shared contexts in literature teaching. Inspired by White's (2011) study, I explored some of these topics, including values awareness though aesthetic experience, in Think it Through: Fostering Aesthetic Experiences to Raise Interest in Literature at the High School Level, published in the *Journal of the Canadian Association of Curriculum Studies* (2015). My doctoral project focuses on high school students' aesthetic experiences in response to literature and film adaptations, and whether the latter provides an enhanced experience of the text-based medium. Boyd White's introduction to aesthetic experiences has come a long way, and made me want to go further in research investigations exploring these implications. The perspectives we provide in this book are the result of many years of research conducted by Boyd White and me.

Amélie Lemieux

Concluding Note

This text is intended to spur interest in the fostering of aesthetic experience and to provide a strategy for an understanding of the patterns we individually create to arrive at those experiences. It is our hope that this text will assist teachers, students, and anyone else interested in how we make significant meaning of our interactions with our world. Why is that a useful endeavour? The short answer is that such study provides an essential counter-balance to the emphasis on de-personalized education (standardization), on information and skills deemed essential to competition in the global markets—in short, on learning "from the neck up." In other words, aesthetic education draws attention to that which is personally significant, sensuously as well as reflexively experienced. That is, I argue that aesthetically funded encounters are central to any concept of holistic education, formal and informal, insofar as they involve the whole person, intellectually, affectively, and physically.

SECTION ONE

CHAPTER ONE

Epistemological and Ontological Stances

AMÉLIE LEMIEUX AND BOYD WHITE

In this chapter, we provide a brief overview of phenomenological principles as they have developed since the beginning of the twentieth century. Then we discuss our rationale for the application of some of those principles to explore personal accounts of meaning-making, particularly in relation to the reading of literary artworks.[1] Optimally, we hope to foster aesthetic experiences achieved through the reading of literature.

PHENOMENOLOGICAL ORIENTATIONS

Edmund Husserl (1859–1938) is generally considered to be the father of 20th century phenomenology. It was his position that human certainties are only achieved through individual experiences of the world, and that these experiences originate, take form, and materialize in and through one's consciousness. Phenomenology, therefore, is the study of human consciousness. Put another way, phenomenology is the scientific study of the essential structures of experience—experience that "points essentially to referents beyond itself" (Spiegelberg, 1975, p. 248). Those referents can take many forms—cultural norms, personal beliefs, memories, et cetera—layers of influences upon any given experience. That is, phenomenology is not bound by empirical facts. Rather, it is concerned with fundamental relationships between an experiencing subject (a person) and objects of that experience—with *how* objects are experienced, rather than *why*. Husserl's rationale was that the perspective useful to the natural sciences, what he called the "natural standpoint," is not applicable to the study of human psychology because of the variability of human experience. The natural standpoint assumes a continuity of experience; for example, an empirical measurement today will be the same tomorrow. That is, in the empirical sciences, the objective emphasis assumes the existence and acceptance of a permanent, stable, external world, one that has quantitative properties, and in which standards of truth and falsity apply. From that perspective laws of causal relationships may be established. Husserl was intent on the study of experience as free as possible from such everyday, objectively oriented presuppositions. For, as the word implies, "experience" is fundamentally subjective. Husserl's orientation was essentially epistemological. That is, his focus on human experience was ultimately concerned with the study of *how* we make meaning. And meaning is experienced, not as a concrete measurable object, but as a synthesis of discrete acts of direct, subjective experiencing, which, in turn, is influenced by antecedent beliefs (*doxa*)[2] regarding the nature of the world. Pursuing this line of thought, Thomas Groenewald (2004) reminds us that the aim of phenomenology is to "describe as accurately as possible [a] phenomenon" (p. 5) *as-experienced*. Husserl was intent on arriving at the essence of phenomena, that is, what all experiences of a particular phenomenon have in common.

Many phenomenologists today consider the pursuit of essences to be idealistic. Those practitioners have tended to move from an epistemological stance (the study of the nature of knowledge) to more of an ontological one (the study of being, existence, and reality). Our approach takes the middle ground. That is, we do attempt to find common themes within the experiences of our participants while at the same time acknowledging their ontological, idiosyncratic "being" or selfhood. For the purposes of this book, we rely extensively on Linda Finlay's (2012) definition:

> Phenomenological research characteristically starts with concrete descriptions of lived situations, often first-person accounts, set down in everyday language and avoiding abstract intellectual generalizations. The researcher proceeds by reflectively analyzing these descriptions, perhaps idiographically first, then by offering a synthesized account, for example, identifying general themes about the essence of the phenomenon. (p. 21)

In practice, when teachers-researchers ask students to describe or report their individual experiences in relation to phenomena such as novels, the nature of the exercise becomes phenomenological. That is, research grounded in phenomenological inquiry shares ties with "the lived experiences of the people involved … with the issue that is being researched." (Groenewald, 2004, p. 5)

PHENOMENOLOGICAL HERMENEUTICS AND READING

In Louise Rosenblatt's (1978) transactional theory of reading she argues: "in aesthetic reading, the reader's attention is centred directly on what he is living through during his relationship with that particular text" (p. 25). That notion of "living through" has ontological overtones, a way of being in the world, which brings us to phenomenological hermeneutics. As Max van Manen (2014) explains: "Phenomenology becomes hermeneutical when its method is taken to be essentially interpretive ... [as opposed to descriptive]" (p. 132). However, "whatever appears in consciousness is already the work of the constituting ego (subjectivity). And in this constitution process, *the interpretive is already at work*" (van Manen, 2014, p. 137, our emphasis). Linda Finlay's (2012) definition of hermeneutical phenomenology seems to go in the same direction:

> Interpretation is inevitable and necessary because phenomenology is concerned with meanings, which tend to be implicit and/or hidden. Interpretation is thus centrally involved in unveiling hidden meanings (rather than being a process whereby external frames of reference are brought in and imposed). That we make a transition from actual experience to a second-hand explication indicates a level of translation and interpretation is involved. (p. 23)

And so, humans seek to explain, communicate, and give meaning to their lived experiences through a medium that is often oral or written language. In our case, the exercise of recollecting experiences through verbal or written expression is twofold:

> Textual activity is ... the phenomenological *and* hermeneutical study of human existence: phenomenology because it is the descriptive study of human experience (phenomena) in the attempt to enrich lived experience by mining its meaning; hermeneutics because it is the interpretive study of the expressions and objectifications (texts) of lived experience in the attempt to determine the meaning embodied in them (van Manen, 1990, p. 38, our emphasis).

In a similar vein, in their introductory remarks, Patrick Slattery, Karen Krasny, and Michael Patrick O'Malley (2007) note that notable philosophers and social scientists (such as Hegel, Rorty, Gadamer, and Bakhtin) are in agreement that "all human endeavors involve hermeneutic interpretation" (p. 538). The authors provide a succinct overview of six forms of hermeneutic study and then argue in favour of their own "dialogic hermeneutics" as a reasonable extension of those earlier models. Their slant on hermeneutics calls attention to imagination, creativity, aesthetics, ambiguity, all in the service of a more democratic, humanizing curricular practice. Our own project has strong affinities with those authors' approach.

THE LIMITATIONS OF TRADITIONAL HERMENEUTICS

Paul Ricoeur (1981) defines hermeneutics as the "theory of the operations of understanding in their relation to the interpretation of texts" (p. 43). In other words, it is how meaning-making operates when we read a text. The meaning of the text has a referential dimension, which unfolds in the process of individual interpretation. For example, when a person reads how Jean Des Esseintes describes one of Gustave Moreau's paintings in Huysmans's (1884/2009) novel *Against the Grain* (*À Rebours*), interpretation infuses that person's imagination, which, in turn, is initiated by her or his reading experience of the text:

> Des Esseintes had acquired his two masterpieces and, at night, used to sink into revery before one of them—a representation of Salome, conceived in this fashion: A throne, resembling the high altar of a cathedral, reared itself beneath innumerable vaults leaping from heavy Romanesque pillars, studded with polychromatic bricks, set with mosaics, incrusted with lapis lazuli and sardonyx, in a palace that, like a basilica, was at once Mohammedan and Byzantine in design. (p. 76)

What we have argued is that, through reading the same narrative description, each reader's referents differ. As we saw with the contributions of phenomenology, the mental images that a reader creates of the Romanesque pillars and mosaics are uniquely that person's, and we cannot see into another's imagined images (unless of course that person shares her often limited perceptual accounts through another limited medium that is language). That is why we think that, by stimulating our imagination through reading, we tackle a locus of interpretation that is ours, in which the relationship between subject and object takes place (Dewey, 1943; Eisner, 1998; Rosenblatt, 1978). As Probst (1990) argues: "Literary texts are not, however, the repositories of meaning; rather, they are a source of intellectual, emotional, and aesthetic experience, out of which meaning may be made by the individual reader." (p. 30) And these meanings are negotiated in social contexts with peers and the teacher (Fish, 1980). As Hans Georg Gadamer (1975) notes, interpretation of text may be bound by our perspectives (our *prejudices*—in his terms), but it remains a social act because we are influenced by the points of view of others: "we [must] remain open to the meaning of the other person or of the text. But this openness always includes our own meanings or ourselves in relation to it." (p. 238)

There are reasons why we do not fully adopt traditional hermeneutics. The first one is that Gadamerian hermeneutics imply that there is *a* truth to be decoded from the text, and respects the principle that such textual truths even exist. That is, for Gadamer (1975), textual interpretation is bound by one's "prejudices" (Gadamer's term, which has negative connotations. We prefer "bias," which can be positive or negative), which do not hinder the interpretation act *per se*, but constitute a necessary condition for interpretation to happen. According to Gadamer, one must acknowledge one's prejudices to extract the "true" meaning of the text: "The important thing is to be aware of one's own bias, so that the text may present itself in all its newness and thus be able to assert its own truth against one's own fore-meanings" (p. 238). Gadamer's stance seems effective in theory, but to apply it in classroom practice seems difficult, unless it be introduced with measures that make these biases easily identifiable for the reader. We could think of reading logs or the procedures of *aesthetigram-making*. In the next chapter, we will provide an example where a student became aware of her biases upon initial encounters with an artwork, and through that awareness was able to enlarge upon her subsequent aesthetic experience of that same artwork.

RATIONALE

In our opening paragraph in this chapter, we stated that we hoped to foster aesthetic experiences through the reading of literature. Before we can consider that possibility, however, we need to investigate how meaning making emerges from reading. In other words, we need to apply Groenewald's directive—to describe the experience as accurately as possible. In Chapter 2, we will provide an example of such description. But why use phenomenology or its hermeneutic derivations? In this section, we address that question and confine our discussion to a rationale for the methodology we pursue.

To begin, we maintain that a starting point for phenomenological inquiry into meaning making in conjunction with reading literature has two requirements: (1) We need to create conditions where experiences are at the forefront. (2) We need to enable students to develop a heightened awareness of their own experiences. In turn, that awareness becomes the foundation upon which reflection can take place (see White, 2007, 2011, 2013, 2014; White & Lemieux, 2015). As Howard (2002) notes, good phenomenological inquiries always "provide concrete portrayals of lived experience and offer insightful reflections on the meanings of those experiences" (p. 49). In Chapters 2–6 of this text, we have attempted to exemplify that practice.

READING ENGAGEMENT, CONTEXT AND AESTHETIC EXPERIENCE

Individuals have varying stories, backgrounds, bodies, and personalities. It follows that students experience texts differently from one another. The term "individual," from the Latin *dividere* (to divide), and *in* (not) means indivisibility, not, however, isolation. That is, it is possible for multiple beings to experience the same feelings and thoughts when they read, watch a film, listen to music—to share experiences. The reason that we often agree on the meaning of something (for example, "that was a good movie") is that we share substantial contexts with each other. Another example of sharing would be that of the catharsis that might be felt collectively during a classical music concert or a chamber orchestra. The aesthetic reception in these circumstances can often lead to sensorial engagement (e.g., close attention) or expressions (e.g., tears, blinks, and fidgeting). Reacting through stimulated senses is typical of the human race. Most of us have aesthetic experiences on occasion. When they take place, they have the capacity to enrich our lives insofar as they provide a particular significance to the occasion.

Let us take the reading of literature as an example. Lived experiences, or *Erfarhung* (van Manen, 1990), of reading literature in classroom contexts might give indications of reading engagement when the reader feels immersed in the text. What does this mean, concretely? To answer this apparently simple, yet complex question, we argue that reading engagement depends on the moments where one feels drawn to the characters or events. When the reader is really immersed in the drama, the act of turning the novel's pages goes unnoticed. The physical and mental acts of reading become subsumed within the more engrossing act of entering into the story. "In reading a novel or a poem I forget who I am, I am now the one who lives in the text" (van Manen, 2002, p. 251). Csikszentmihalyi & Robinson (1990) refer to this phenomenon as a "flow" experience—see also Maxime Greene's "wide awakeness" (1977, 1995). We consider the terms "living," "engagement," "flow," and "wide awakeness" to be synonymous.

But levels of engagement vary, just as readers experience texts differently. Rosenblatt (1978) notes two reading stances as part of her transaction theory of reading: (1) the efferent stance, which elicits information and factual details emerging from the text; (2) the aesthetic stance (the focus of our work) whereby lived-through experiences of the reading scenario take place. High levels of engagement occur when readers activate their aesthetic stance, as prompted by reader-response exercises and activities or by their own natural narrative imagination (See Nussbaum, 1998).

Rosenblatt's (1978) and van Manen's (2002) statements on living-through the story are obviously ideals, but not necessarily unrealistic goals. Some readers do undergo such reading experiences. However, we do not have to stretch these statements to the extent that one has to *live through the text* to be engaged in reading, and the reason for this is that readers perceive art or literary works differently and have different levels of engagement depending on their attitudes, interests, experiences—their *vécu*. As an example, 15-year-old Oliver, who has affinities with literature (e.g., he enjoys reading and writing outside of the classroom) and who can identify with a character of the plot, will not experience the narrative the same way as Julie, a 16-year-old who reads only fashion blogs, or with 16-year-old Michael, who likes mathematics and does not like English class because of personal tensions with his teacher. This standpoint is not new (cf. Stanley Fish's community of readers, 1980; Louise Rosenblatt, 1991; or more recently, Marion

Sauvaire's notion of *sujet divers*, 2010), and comes from a long tradition of recognition of the primacy of individual experience, as Rosenblatt's (1969) compelling example illustrates: "To ask someone else to experience a work of art for him would be tantamount to seeking nourishment by asking someone else to eat his dinner for him" (p. 39). Our point is that subjective experience is one's primary source of understanding. And although we may share contexts to varying degrees, no one's life is identical to another's. It follows that the meanings we derive from our individual experiences will, to at least some degree, be idiosyncratic. This variability is what gives our social lives its richness and, of course, a main source of disagreement about the meaning of a shared phenomenon. For teachers, that variability presents special challenges.

A FEW NOTES ON EVALUATION

One of those challenges has to do with assessment. That is, if students do not all arrive at the same meaning from an assigned text, how is the teacher to assess their learning (Bayard, 2011)? How much credit should teachers assign to subjective interpretation as opposed to that given for what philosopher, novelist, and literary critic Umberto Eco (1985) referred to as the *rights of the text?* As Bayard explained, varying phenomenological interpretations of text present a quandary for some, given the presumed discrepancy between the author's text and the reader's interpretations:

> "The literary text is confronted with a readership that is ill-prepared to understand its complexity, a readership that possesses such a distant cultural capital compared to that of the author's. Thus, another text immediately replaces the literary text, as if the teacher and students, separated by the paradigms discussed by Kuhn, lived in worlds made different by age, cultural background, social context, or knowledge of the language." (p. 14)

If Bayard's commentary is intended to dispel notions of the possibility of a universal truth within any literary passage, his example is a good one. Nonetheless, the description seems an extreme vision of the differences between author and readers. For example, certainly our lives today are different from what they would have been in Shakespeare's time. But we still read or attend his plays. Undoubtedly, there are differences between the way we assign meanings to the plays today and the way audiences responded in his time. But the contexts of comedy and tragedy, the human condition, nonetheless enable shared experiences. What do the differences and the shareability have to do with learning assessment in the literature classroom? Are we forced to limit our testing to what can be gleaned from efferent reading, in other words, to information that is easily testable? And what would students gain from such tests?

Alan Purves, Theresa Rogers, and Anna Soter (1990), dedicated an entire chapter in their text, *How porcupines make love II: A study of response to literature*, to assignments and feedback in their pivotal work on reader-response. In Chapter 11, titled "How can a poor little literature program survive in that great big world of tests?," the authors stated that the main problem with standardized tests (assessing knowledge of assumed irrevocable truths) in literature teaching is that "they tend to kill off everything that we suggest should be nurtured." (p. 161) And that "everything," we suggest, has to do with developing in students an awareness of what it means to be human—and how literature can provide guidelines to that awareness. Standardized testing, as useful as it may be for checking factual detail, will not take us there. Attention to the subjective nature of engaged reading just might, however difficult it may be to put such assessment into practice. Purves, Rogers, and Soter (1990) offer some suggestions in that regard. Specifically, they list eight main criteria for grading students' phenomenologically funded reading responses (pp. 172–173). The criteria presuppose that students can be guided towards addressing certain questions:

Criterion	Questions for Evaluation
(1) *Re-creating*	Is the reader's recreation (or performance) of events compatible with that of the original work in terms of its plot, events, protagonists?
(2) *Valuing*	Can the reader articulate his thoughts independently, without an overpowering influence from the teacher or his peers?
(3) *Generalizing*	Can the reader distinguish generalizations from stereotypes? Is she immersed in subjective or objective thinking, or can she dare express generalizations?
(4) *Evaluating*	Can the student go beyond statements like "it is good because I liked it"?
(5) *Interpreting*	Is the student able to express his own epistemological stances?
(6) *Analyzing*	What is the student's analytical potential? For example, how does he elicit distinctions between parts and whole?
(7) *Describing the result of envisioning*	What is the depth of the reader's description as she envisions it?
(8) *Personalizing*	Is the student able to make visceral connections between the text and her or his personal lived experiences, and is s/he stating the repercussions of the work on her or his life?

While not extensive, these parameters offer a strong counter-argument to the contention that subjectivity can't (and even shouldn't) be measured in literature classes. What Purves, Rogers, and Soter provide is a feasible model for the development of practical questions that are relevant for assessing knowledge growth without reliance on single "right" answers.

In contrast to the above example, in Quebec, as elsewhere in North America, learning is assessed largely on the basis of standardized tests. This practice applies to the literature curriculum as well. (In Quebec these tests are called épreuves uniques uniformes). If teachers were to adopt Purves, Rogers, and Soter's reading-response approach and its emphasis on more individualized testing, what resistance might they encounter within the education community, including their fellow teachers? One argument would be that no one has the time or resources to channel the ephemeral reactions of their students, and that, anyway, questions regarding one's aesthetic experiences are seldom asked in provincial exams (for an extensive discussion on the matter, see Purves, Rogers, & Soter, 1990). Another would be that final ministerial examinations are meant to produce open letters outlining elements of an argumentative text, and that teachers need to prepare their students for these types of assessments. As such, these exercises require more efferent than aesthetic knowledge (Rosenblatt, 1976). Nonetheless, Competency 1 of the MELS French Language Education program (2009) also calls for the reading and appreciation of diverse texts (*Lire et apprécier des textes variés*). While we have reservations about the vague nature of the term "appreciation," we give MELS the benefit of the doubt and assume that appreciation does not have to mean that all students appreciate in identical fashion. If that is the case then appreciation opens a window for investigation into students' phenomenological experiences of texts, as the evaluation criteria include, not only efferent detail, but reader-response commentary, judgement, interpretation, and related strategies. These correspond well with Purves *et al.'s* (1990) evaluation criteria described earlier.

INTERPRETATION, THE TEXT, AND THE READER

Quebec's Ministry of Education (MELS) states: "By respecting the limits of the text, that is, by avoiding attribution of faulty meanings or contradictions, the reader exploits the resources of his objectivity and subjectivity to find personal resonances, or to attribute multiple meanings to the text" (MELS, 2009, p. 178). The phrase "limits of the text" brings us into the realm of hermeneutics and has an interesting parallel in Umberto Eco's (1990) "rights of the text." We acknowledge that the text does have certain "rights." For example, if students misread the title of an artwork and then proceed to interpret the work on the basis of that misreading, they trample on those rights. MELS puts it more gently when they speak of "limits" of the text. They also acknowledge the legitimacy of personal resonances and multiple meanings. So, here they support the case for aesthetic reading.

In reference to Eco's use of the rights-of-the-text phrase, Guillemette and Cossette (2006) note:

> The text has rights, and aberrant decodings do occur ... The text may, however, convey (actualisable) elements of which the author was unaware, and still result in interpretive cooperation that has a happy end. (Eco, 1985, 73–74). (n.p.)

The authors' statement addresses the crux of the matter. That is, it is hard to argue against Eco's insistence that while readings are fallible, nonetheless readers tend to concur in their general interpretations, if not in the personal significance of those interpretations. Eco (1990) provided an admittedly bizarre example:

> If Jack the Ripper told us that he did what he did on the grounds of his interpretation of the Gospel according to Saint Luke, I suspect that many reader-oriented critics would be inclined to think that he read Saint Luke in a pretty preposterous way. Non-reader-oriented critics would say that Jack the Ripper was deadly mad—and I confess that, even though feeling very sympathetic with the reader oriented paradigm ... I would agree that Jack the Ripper needed medical care. (p. 144)

Nonetheless, Eco acknowledged that normally the text and the reader have to work in conjunction with one another. The text is essentially "a lazy machine that demands the bold cooperation of the reader to fill in a whole series of gaps" of unsaid or already said missing elements (translation of Eco, 1985, 29, in Guillemette & Cossette, 2006). Further, Eco proposed to differentiate between an "empirical reader" and a "model reader." The former could be said to correspond to Rosenblatt's efferent reader, that is, one who reads pragmatically for data. The latter brings her social and cultural context to work—to fill in the gaps of which Eco spoke. To conclude this section it is worth emphasizing that Eco supported the reader-oriented paradigm.

INTER-SUBJECTIVITY

Above, we discussed the unfortunate consequences of exclusive reliance upon standardized tests in the teaching of literature. We acknowledge, however, that such tests can play a useful role if used judiciously. That is, textual facts can, and should, be favoured over instances of solipsism. But what keeps teachers and educational researchers from investigating reading *experiences* as a starting point for interpretation? Is it not Roland Barthes (1976) who posited: "the object I read is founded by my intention to read: it is simply *legendum*, to be read, issuing from a phenomenology, not from a semiology" (p. 34)? What are the implications of that quotation? To answer that question we must return momentarily to an important feature of phenomenology, that is, to inter-subjectivity.

As we suggested earlier in our introduction to phenomenology, the phenomenologist's emphasis is on experience, not on phenomena independent of the self. Phenomenology, in other words, depends on a radical subjectivity. The data, the phenomenon-as-experienced, is *self-evident*. And because we have the world in common, and meanings evolve out of our interactions with this world, it is possible to share meanings. That is, phenomenologists share descriptions (distribute meanings)—inter-subjectively—from one subject to another, unlike the natural sciences, which operate on the basis of a subject/object perspective. We will return to the educational challenges inherent in inter-subjectivity shortly.

First, in support of the previous paragraph, and to counter the allegations of solipsism in reader-response, we look to David Abram's (1996) commentary on Edmund Husserl's (1960) late multi-subjective turn. He explained: "… the phenomenological field … contains many *other* bodies … The field of appearances, while still a thoroughly subjective realm, [is] inhabited by *multiple* subjectivities; … a collective landscape, constituted by other experiencing subjects as well as by oneself" (p. 37, author's emphasis). In an educational, research-applied context, White (2014) recently studied examples of subjective poetic accounts in response to visual artworks and found that phenomenological written accounts of experience as components of reader-response "provide opportunities for sharing, offering pathways for others' interactions (White, 2014, p. 49).

Above, we alluded to the educational challenges that the radical subjectivity of phenomenology creates. It bears repeating that the only way we can confirm our experiences of the world is to verify them with each other. Inter-subjectivity presupposes that dialogue. We argue, then, that phenomenological exercises in the classroom should be followed, or even preceded, by the sharing of experiences between peers. When those moments take place, the text is "treated not as a sacred object (object of a philology), but essentially as a space of language, as the site of an infinite number of digressions" (Barthes, 1976, p. 28). This way of discussing experiences of the narrative still allows for phenomenological accounts, all the while mediating experiences with the *Other*, without falling into standardized (and standardizing) objectivity: "We need to give room to multiple perspectives to denote meaning from various angles. In other words, it is a matter of being able to handle several ways of seeing as a series of differing views rather than reducing all views to a single correct one" (Eisner, 1998, p. 49). Allowing spaces for these varying reading experiences is important. Who, other than the reader, experiences them? And why should meaning be imposed by someone else? The phenomenological hermeneutic tangent will attempt to answer to this. (We will come back to this shortly.)

We have shown that phenomenology presents a number of advantages and limitations. We highlighted the insights it offers on the experiences of student readers and its potential to inform teachers and researchers regarding felt reading experiences. Then, in terms of challenges, we mentioned the problems it might cause for evaluation in terms of taking into account all the layers embedded in one's subjective moments. Some might say that phenomenology adds no practical value because it highlights experiences that cannot be generalized, thereby creating challenges in assessment and classroom/workload time management. Such activities can indeed appear to be time consuming and unknown territory for some. Nevertheless, phenomenology shows promising avenues for insights into human consciousness (Abram, 1996; Bodgan, 1992; van Manen, 1990; White, 2013, 2014) and showcase *life as lived* (van Manen, 1990). Human experiences determine the framework for phenomenological studies, not the contrary, and the point of collecting stories about other people's experiences is to "become more experienced ourselves" (van Manen, 1990, p. 62). Beach (1990) elaborated on this point:

> Literary texts evoke meanings associated with familiar emotions … For example, in reading a description of a character experiencing the death of a spouse, readers *imagine* that character's grief, thus gaining an understanding of the nature of bereavement. At the same time, by relating their own emotional experiences of grief to the text, they *gain insight* into the character's grief. (p. 69, our emphasis)

IMAGINATION AND INTER-SUBJECTIVITY

Imagining and *gaining insight* are two human activities we must take into consideration where the notions of subjectivity and phenomenology arise. "These are entirely *my* images, *my* phantasies and fears, *my* dreamings … phenomena that arise only for me—images that arise, as it were, on this side of my body" (Abram, 1996, p. 38, author's emphasis). Thus, when reading, the subject-as-self perceives elements according to several factors, be it her mood, background, origins, emotional state, and so forth. Within this framework of experiences, the subject opens a path for transaction with the text, and constructs meaning within that unique personal transaction (Rosenblatt, 1969, 1976). Nonetheless, we are aware that the self operates with other selves in societal contexts where experiences are shared through language (Fish, 1980). In regard to that sharing, Martha Nussbaum (1998) speaks of the importance of having a narrative imagination—for its capacity to engender empathy for others and, in turn, develop a sense of moral responsibility towards the plight of others.

FURTHER NOTES ON READING ENGAGEMENT

We suggested earlier that all phenomenological writings or accounts are hermeneutical. That is, students must interpret their own reading experiences (not just the text itself) and express them to the best of their writing abilities. Our point is that, to understand students' reading engagement we need to go *beyond* the classical notion of hermeneutics that situates meaning-making in the text: "Events find their meaning in aesthetic encounters where knowledge is constructed and reconstructed in every unique situation" (Slattery, Krasny, & O'Malley, 2007, p. 550). Furthermore, "If reading takes on such a determinant role in students' success, we should perhaps empower students in their learning through reader subjectivity" (Lemieux, 2015, p. 69). Then too, it seems reasonable to think of reading engagements as singular, aesthetically oriented *events*. To explore those events, questions we might ask are: What are students' individual reading experiences of such and such book? How does affect manifest itself in students' reading responses? What is the nature of aesthetic experiences in reading engagement? That is, what do the experiences consist of? Such questions take us beyond a strictly hermeneutic framework towards more of a mixed hermeneutic phenomenological account. As White and Tompkins (2005) noted: "Student interactions with artworks are inextricably linked with their abilities to articulate those experiences ... the search for the right words drives the meaning of the encounter as much as art-directed perceptions do" (p. 6). In short, when we interpret the text (hermeneutics) and when we develop articulations or descriptions of that interpretation process, the latter are most likely going to be phenomenological as they aim at elucidating lived experience (van Manen, 1990, 2002, 2007, 2014).

As we saw, students' reading experiences count as phenomenological, whether they be positive, negative, or variable. As White (2014) observed, an encounter with art "may vary from person to person and from one time to another for the same person, but the variable moments nonetheless add up to a phenomenon classifiable as aesthetic experience" (p. 36).[3] The essence of these experiences remains phenomenological. Therefore, our focus is on investigating individual experiences and what they mean for readers. The plethora of possible various experiences do not, however, necessarily suggest engagement. Boredom, for example, is an experience, but it is surely not a sign of engagement. For instance, a teacher might assign George Orwell's *1984* to his grade 11 class, but it is not a given that all students will engage with the narrative. We all know the repercussions of non-engagement[4] in reading, which can be felt at the levels of the global economy, culture, and society (National Endowment for the Arts, 2007).

Like Louise Rosenblatt (1976), Dennis Sumara (2002) demonstrated how readers' engagement with literary texts might open the path to conditions for developing insight into human experiences, and how teachers might bolster these interpretive attitudes in the classroom. Despite major advancements with reader-response methods that foster phenomenological accounts, he acknowledged that close reading, a strategy that dictates that truth is inherent in the text (i.e., non-phenomenological), is still applied in Canadian high schools. As he explained:

"Although students are asked to consider the literary text 'open' when they respond personally, they are also asked to consider it 'closed' when they are asked to identify, with certainty, the main conflict, or the protagonist's tragic flaw" (Sumara, 2002, p. 33). The tension between phenomenology and hermeneutics is highly palpable in the pedagogical situation that Sumara described. Through our individual journeys as educators and researchers, we have witnessed similar situations. To alleviate that tension, and more precisely, to foster subjective interpretations of text, in Sumara' text, *Why Reading Literature in School Still Matters* (2002), he addressed the awareness of the body and the self when reading, and how our biological self is responsible for our interpretations of text:

> The work of art creates a gathering location for the usually unnoticed relationships between the biological and the phenomenological. Making a novel, a painting, a memoir, reading fiction, writing essays—all these create possible conditions where troubling bodies collect to engage in the necessary work of interpretation. (p. 46)

CHALLENGES OF PHENOMENOLOGICAL HERMENEUTICS AND PROPOSED SOLUTIONS

The challenges of phenomenological hermeneutics are multi-layered and complex. First, one might argue that not all text interpretations are valid, as Eco's Jack-the-Ripper story illustrates. The hermeneutical phenomenology of reader-response is fallible, especially to those researchers who see this epistemology as being too relativistic. But it is only fair to acknowledge that even in empirical studies, it is possible to be wrong. However, there is a word in phenomenology—apodictic—which means the impossibility of being wrong, or beyond dispute, or clearly provable and logically certain/incontestable. For example: 2 + 2 = 4; the existence of gravity. Both statements may be said to be apodictic. For our purposes, the fact of the existence of individual experiences (of reading) is apodictic.

As Slattery, Krasny, & O'Malley (2007) reminded us, "the complexity of understanding aesthetic experiences is difficult to those committed to a modern mechanistic understanding where such experiences do not conform to the logic of positivism, behaviourism, rationalism, and structural analysis." (p. 551) If students are required to answer questions that stimulate their efferent readings of texts (i.e. information about the text), then of course, asking them to develop their understanding through their reactions to the text seems unconnected to the task at hand. We argue, on the contrary, that being connected to, and aware of, oneself is a promising way to becoming engaged in reading. We acknowledge that aesthetically-funded knowledge can be *aided by* contextual knowledge (Carroll, 2001, 2002; Eco, 1985; Lemieux, 2015; White & Tompkins, 2005; White, 2011,

2013). Usually, the more we know about a topic, the deeper and more authentic our levels of engagement are likely to be. We emphasize how crucial it is that students get the basic, empirically verifiable information right (e.g., that Sally, not John, drove off the cliff). Otherwise, any ensuing aesthetic engagement will be distorted by faulty information. But such information is just a starting point to any authentic engagement in reading. It is also important to acknowledge that the reader should not impose herself—her ideologies—on the work. This is the point of Susan Sontag's (1966) essay *Against interpretation.* It is important to note that Sontag was not against all interpretation, just that which was dogmatic and stifling, as ideologies tend to be.

A second challenge that phenomenological hermeneutics invites is the question of the extent to which knowledge of others and of the self is possible. Holland (1998) argued that it is impossible to completely know oneself and others: "One can never know a self, including one's own, except through the processes of perception shaped by one's self ... One cannot, therefore, have perfect knowledge of others' selves or one's own" (p. 1209). (See also Emmanuel Levinas (1906–1995). Levinas argued that we can never truly know an Other. His view is in opposition to Martin Buber's *I – Thou I* aspirations.) The significance of Levinas' and Holland's position has to do with definitions of engagement. That is, to what extent does one become the character in a story? Does one always maintain a degree of separation (e.g., knowledge that one is only reading a book after all, not really driving over a cliff)?

Although Holland (1998) and Hirsch (1979) come from two different and opposed traditions, the former being reader-response, the latter being New Criticism, it seems as though Holland's statement towards knowledge of the self and others echo Hirsch's (1979) position in *Validity in Interpretation*: "I can never know another person's intended meaning with certainty because I cannot get inside his head to compare the meaning he intends with the meaning I understand, and only by such direct comparison would I be certain that his meaning and my own are identical" (p. 17). Hirsch (1979) would particularly take issue with our take on phenomenological hermeneutics, for he posited: "whenever a meaning is attached to a sequence of words it is impossible to escape an author" (p. 5). His statement and school of thought is strongly opposed to Barthes' (1968) position in *Death of the Author*, which encourages readers to explore their perceptions rather than the author's life and background (for this very reason, some hailed Barthes' position as the "Birth of the reader"). Phenomenological hermeneutics might then be incompatible with those forms of inquiry that involve closed systems, such as textual investigations that excavate exclusive value in the author's "intended" meaning.

Max van Manen (2014) has identified a third difficulty inherent in phenomenological hermeneutics in his text *Phenomenology of Practice*. That is, he remarked on the challenge emerging from attempts to describe lived experiences, for their character is ephemeral and elusive. In that regard, van Manen (2014) asked: "If I focus on an experience that strikes me as particularly interesting but that is not easy to be captured in language, then I may wonder: what word(s) do I use to describe this experience?" (p. 242) He noted the fleeting character of experiences that, at times, may go beyond language. In other words, standard descriptions can sometimes hardly do justice to the complexity of lived experiences. This fact poses a very important challenge to phenomenology.

In response to these challenges, we adopt White's (1998, 2007, 2011, 2013, 2014) strategy of researching lived experience through aesthetigrams. Over the past two decades, his work with students and pre-service teachers has shown that there is a way to capture, recollect, and describe the fleeting loci of experiences, and to place these individual moments of experience into categories. Over the years, White (2011) and his students have developed an extensive list of more than fifty potential categories and subcategories of experience. The list keeps expanding and was used in a recent study in literature pedagogy and reading interest in literature (Lemieux, 2015). This approach is an initial step in addressing the difficulty of describing experiences to which van Manen (2014) alluded. For example, a proposed subcategory of the "feelings" category reads as "an overall feeling regardless of your inability to pinpoint the cause(s) or to attach a precise label to the feeling" (White, 2011, annex). This openness to multiple types of experiences—and plural possibilities to express their essence—serves well to counter the limitations of everyday language. White (2013) has asserted that aesthetigrams do help students realize the complexities of their individual private encounters, but that this realization is only an initial step in their efforts to describe their experiences. The next step is to produce a narrative of that experience, either through the standard essay format or, for those who want to emphasize the affective nature of the encounter, more poetic interpretations According to White (2013), most students rely on the former. Students are familiar with essay writing, much less so with poetry.

In a recent article titled *Student Generated Art Criticism*, White (2014) further addressed the pedagogical limitations of phenomenology in his work on pre-service teachers' interactions with visual artworks. While acknowledging that varying perspectives of the works cause challenges in the classroom, he sees these different points of view as beneficial to, rather than impeding, meaning-making and engagement. On this matter, White (2014) explained:

> Variability presents a pedagogical challenge; differences in approach, viewpoint, and degree of impact are likely. Thus an instructor is obligated to accommodate, even encourage, multiple understandings while insisting on evidence for an individual's stance. *Arrival at some commonly agreed-upon truth is not the issue here.* Rather, it has more to do with developing a tolerance for ambiguity, to increased clarity and personal significance insofar as the encounter reinforces one's understanding and contributes to self-knowledge. (p. 37, our emphasis)

White (2014) did not suggest that arriving at an agreed-upon truth is impossible, as we do share many contexts. Indeed, for something to have personal significance, it must have a ring of truth about it—corresponding to the reader's understanding of some components of life as she lives it. Seamus Heaney, in his 1995 Nobel Lecture, provides an eloquent example. He credits poetry "for its truth to life" (n.p.). He gives the example of Homer's *Fall of Troy:*

> At the sight of the man panting and dying there,
> she slips down to enfold him, crying out;
> then feels the spears, prodding her back and shoulders,
> and goes bound into slavery and grief.
> Piteous weeping wears away her cheeks:
> But no more piteous than Odysseus' tears,
> Cloaked as they were now, from the company. (n.p.)

Engaged readers can surely identify with the wife of the dying soldier, with her grief and that of Odysseus. Those readers also recognize poem's capacity "to possess a concrete reliability" (n.p.) in its depiction of the cruelty of war. In short, readers today share contexts—of love, grief, war, and more—with people of 2500 years ago. We recognize truth when we concretely experience it, despite our possible multiple perspectives. But the issue is not the intent of the author (Barthes, 1977); the issue is readers' capacities to respond.

CONCLUDING REMARKS

In this chapter, we introduced phenomenological concepts to address the study of readers' aesthetic responses to texts. Phenomenology is "rooted in exploration" (Marshall, 2010, p. 82)—in our work, exploration and description of the lived experience of reading. We have described strategies such as the use of aesthetigrams to assist in phenomenological explorations and suggested the benefits and challenges inherent in our approach. The benefits include awareness of the range of influences and activities that take place during engaged reading. That awareness may enable teachers to develop strategies to increase engagement on the part of less-engaged readers. Limitations of a phenomenological epistemology include: (1) the challenges inherent in assessing the validity of reader response in an assessment-driven setting such as the language arts classroom; (2) generalizing the findings to cater to broader research contributions.

Through our perspective on hermeneutics and phenomenological hermeneutics, we showed that the description of lived experiences of reading can be more complex than it may initially seem. The primary reason for this might be that the negotiation space in which the mind decides what words to describe the experiences can sometimes be incommensurate with the felt experience itself. That is, sometimes standard vocabulary will not suffice. Nevertheless, studies conducted by White (2007, 2011, 2013, 2014) show promising avenues to address the ability to faithfully describe moments of experience through aesthetigrams and subsequent evocative writings. Another example, based on White's model, is Lemieux's (2015) study on high school students' moment-by-moment reactions to literature. We will describe in detail examples of this method in Chapters 2–6.

Like phenomenological accounts of reading, hermeneutics cause other interpretative problems such as the validity of textual interpretations (mainly because several author-oriented researchers argue that truth resides in the text rather than in the reader's interpretations of that text). On the other hand, hermeneutics allow for the investigation of encounters through student-oriented writings on reactions to a narrative and understandings of reader engagement. In that sense, it does help fill the function of drawing contours for reading engagement.

NOTES

1. Readers can find a parallel study in White's (2009) *Aesthetics Primer* and in Chapter 2 in this text where the focus is largely on visual art.
2. A Husserlian concept: our perceptions are influenced by our beliefs.
3. Eaton and Moore (2002) refer to the layering-up phenomenon as *sorites*. They use the typical example of grains of sand. Each grain is individual, but at some point, together, they become a heap. In parallel, individual experiential moments are simply what they are—memories, judgements, perceptions, and so forth—but combined, they may constitute an aesthetic experience.
4. As opposed to disengagement in reading. That is, non-engaged readers are not engaged in (or are uncommitted to) the act of reading. They are indifferent to the activity. Disengaged readers are not indifferent, but for whatever reasons, they actively separate themselves from the activity of reading.

REFERENCES

Abbs, P. (1991). Defining the aesthetic field. In R. A. Smith and A. Simpson (Eds.), *Aesthetics and Arts Education* (pp. 245–255). Urbana and Chicago, IL: University of Illinois Press.

Abram, D. (1996). *The spell of the sensuous: Perception and language in a more-than-human world*. New York, NY: Vintage Books.

Ahr, S. & Joole, P. (2013). Transmission et expérience esthétique dans les premier et second degrés. In N. Rannou (Ed.), L'expérience du sujet lecteur: travaux en cours (pp. 133–145). Grenoble, France: Presses de l'Université de Grenoble.

Barthes, R. (1977). The death of the author. In S. Heath, *Image, Music, Text* (pp. 142–148). London: Fontana.

Bayard, P. (2011). Preface. In Mazauric, C., Fourtanier, M. J., & Langlade, G. *Le texte du lecteur* (pp. 12–17). ThéoCrit' vol. 2, Brussels: Peter Lang.

Berleant, A. (2000). *The aesthetic field: A phenomenology of aesthetic experience.* Christchurch, New Zealand: Cybereditions.

Bodgan, D. (1992). *Re-education the imagination: Towards a poetics, politics, and pedagogy of literary engagement.* Portsmouth: Heinemann.

Brehm, S. (2008). Le rôle de l'imaginaire dans le processus de référenciation. *Figura, 20,* 31–44.

Bresler, L. & Macintyre Latta, M. (2008). Venturing into unknown territory: Using aesthetic representations to understand reading comprehension. *International Journal of Education and the Arts, 9*(1), 1–23.

Bressler, C. E. (2011). Literary criticism: An introduction to theory and practice (5th ed.). Upper Saddle River, NJ: Prentice Hall.

Brothers, M. (2014). *Distance in preaching: Room to speak, space to listen.* Grand Rapids, MI: William B. Eerdmans.

Carroll, N. (2001). *Beyond aesthetics: Philosophical essays.* Cambridge: Cambridge University Press.

Csikszentmihalyi, M. (1990). *Flow: The psychology of optimal experience.* San Francisco, CA: Harper Collins.

Csikszentmihalyi, M. & Robinson, R. (1990). *The art of seeing: An interpretation of the aesthetic encounter.* Malibu, CA: J. Paul Getty Trust.

Csikszentmihalyi, M. (2014). Flow: The joy of reading. In M. Csikszentmihalyi, *Applications of flow in human development and education* (pp. 227–240). New York, NY: Springer.

Dewey, J. (1943/1958). *Art as experience.* New York: Capricorn Books.

Dias, P. (1985). Researching reader-response to poetry—Part I: A case for responding-aloud protocols. *English Quarterly, 18*(4), 104–118.

Dias, P. (1986). Researching reader-response to poetry—Part II: What happens when they read a poem. *English Quarterly, 19*(1), 9–21.

Dufays, J.-L. (1994). *Stéréotype et lecture: Essai sur la réception littéraire.* Liège: Mardaga.

Dufays, J.-L. (2007). Le pluriel des réceptions effectives: Débats théoriques et enjeux didactiques. *Littérature (Recherches), 46,* 71–90.

Dufays, J.-L. (2011). Quel enseignement de la lecture et de la littérature à l'heure des « compétences »? *Pratiques, 149–150,* 227–248.

Eaton, M. M. & Moore, R. (2002). Aesthetic experience: Its revival and its relevance to aesthetic education. *Journal of Aesthetic Education, 36*(2), 9–23.

Eco, U. (1985). *Lector in fabula.* Paris: Grasset.

Eisner, E. W. (1998). *The enlightened eye: Qualitative inquiry and the enhancement of educational practice.* Upper Saddle River, NJ: Prentice Hall.

Fenner, D. E. W. (2010). Context building and education imaginative engagement. *Journal of Aesthetic Education, 44*(3), 109–123.

Finlay, L. (2012). Debating phenomenological methods. In N. Friesen, C. Hendriksson, & Saevi, T. (Eds), *Hermeneutic Phenomenology in Education: Method and Practice,* (pp. 17–37). Rotterdam: Sense.

Fish, S. (1980). *Is there a text in this class? The authority of interpretive communities.* Cambridge, MA: Harvard University Press.

Fourtanier, M. J., Langlade, G., & Mazauric, C. (2006). Dispositifs de lecture et formation des lecteurs. *Proceedings of the 7th annual meeting of the Rencontres des Chercheurs en Didactique de la Littérature,* Université de Montpellier.

Gambrell, L. B. & Marinak, B. A. (1997). Incentives and intrinsic motivation to read. *Reading engagement: Motivating readers through integrated instruction* (pp. 205–217). Newark, DE: International Reading Association.

Gardner, H. (1982). *Art, mind, and brain: A cognitive approach to creativity*. New York, NY: Basic Books Publishers.

Graesser, A. C. & D'Mello, S. (2012). Moment-to-moment emotions during reading. *The Reading Teacher, 66*(3), 238–242.

Greene, M. (1977). Toward wide-awakeness: An argument for the arts ands humanities in education. *Teachers College Record, 79*(1), 119–125.

Greene, M. (1991). Aesthetic literacy. In R. A. Smith and A. Simpson (Eds.). *Aesthetics and Arts Education* (pp. 149–161). Urbana and Chicago, IL: University of Illinois Press.

Greene, M. (1995) *Releasing the imagination: Essays on education, the arts and social change*. San Francisco: Jossey-Bass.

Guthrie, J. T. (1996). Educational contexts for engagement in literacy. *The Reading Teacher, 49*(6), 432–445.

Guthrie, J. T., Alverson, S., & Poundstone, C. (1999). Engaging students in reading. *Knowledge Quest, 27*(4), 8–16.

Guthrie, J. T. & Cox, K. E. (2001). Classroom conditions for motivation and engagement in reading. *Educational Psychology Review, 13*(3), 283–302.

Guthrie, J. T. & Knowles, K. T. (2001). Promoting reading motivation. In L. Verhoeven & C. Snow (Eds.). *Literacy and motivation: Reading engagement in individuals and groups* (pp. 159–176). Mahwah, NJ: Lawrence Erlbaum Associates.

Guthrie, J. T., Van Meter, P., Hancock, G. R., McCann, A., Anderson, E., & Alao, S. (1998). Does concept-oriented reading instruction increased strategy use and conceptual learning from text? *Journal of Educational Psychology, 90*(2), 261–278.

Guthrie, J. T. & Wigfield, A. (1997). *Reading engagement: Motivating readers through integrated instruction*. Newark, DE: International Reading Association.

Guthrie, J. T. & Wigfield, A. (2000). Engagement and motivation in reading. In Kamil, M. L., Mosenthal, P. B., Pearson, P. D., & Barr, R. *Handbook of reading research Vol. III* (pp. 403–422). Mahwah, NJ: Lawrence Erlbaum Associates.

Heaney, S. (1995). *Nobel Lecture*. Retrieved from: http://www.nobelprize.org/nobel_prizes/literature/laureates/1995/heaney-lecture.html. Accessed June 28, 2017.

Heffernan, J. (1993). *Museum of words: The poetics of ekphrasis from Homer to Ashbery*. Chicago & London: University of Chicago Press.

Hohendahl, P. U. (1989). *Building a national literature: The case of Germany, 1830–1870*. Ithaca, NY: Cornell University Press.

Holland, N. (1998). Reader-response criticism. *International Journal of Psycho-analysis, 79*(6), 1203–1211.

Howard, P. A. (2002). "The look" in teachers' performance evaluation. In M. Van Manen (Ed.), *Writing in the dark: Phenomenological studies in interpretive inquiry* (pp. 49–60). London, ON: Althouse Press.

Howell, J. S. (2011). Implications of classroom writing instruction emphasizing imagination, creativity, and dialogue: A case study. Unpublished doctoral thesis, Kent State University.

Husserl, E. (1960). Cartesian meditations: An introduction to phenomenology. Translated by Dorion Cairns. The Hague: Martinus Nijhoff Publishers.

Iser, W. (1978). The act of reading: A theory of aesthetic response. Baltimore, MA: Johns Hopkins University Press.

Jauss, H. R. (1978). Pour une esthétique de la réception. Paris: Gallimard.

Jones, R. L. Jr. (1979) Phenomenological balance and aesthetic response. *Journal of Aesthetic Education, 13*(1), 93–106.

Kjeldsen, J. (2001). What can the aesthetic movement tell us about aesthetic education? *Journal of Aesthetic Education, 31*(1), 85–97.

Lacelle, N. & Langlade, G. (2007). Former des lecteurs/spectateurs par la lecture subjective des œuvres. In J.-L. Dufays, Enseigner et apprendre la littérature aujourd'hui pour quoi faire? (pp. 55–65). Louvain-la-Neuve: Presses Universitaires de Louvain.

Lacelle, N. (2009). Modèle de lecture-spectature, à intention didactique, de l'œuvre littéraire et de son adaptation filmique. Thèse inédite. Montréal: Université du Québec à Montréal, Département des sciences de l'éducation.

Lacelle, N. (2012). Des propositions d'enseignement de la lecture littéraire et filmique pour fonder une didactique de la lecture multimodale. In M. Lebrun, N. Lacelle, & J.-F. Boutin (Eds.), La littératie médiatique multimodale: De nouvelles approches en lecture-écriture à l'école et hors de l'école (pp. 171–187). Québec, QC: Presses de l'Université du Québec.

Langer, J. (2001). Literature as an environment for engaged readers. In L. Verhoeven & C. Snow (Eds.), *Literacy and motivation: Reading engagement in individuals and groups* (pp. 177–194). Mahwah, NJ: Lawrence Erlbaum Associates.

Langlade, G. (2004). Sortir du formalisme, accueillir les lecteurs réels. *Le Français aujourd'hui, 145*, 85–96.

Langlade, G. (2006). L'activité fictionnalisante du lecteur. In M. Braud, B. Laville, & B. Louichon (Eds.), *Les enseignements de la fiction* (pp. 163–176). Bordeaux: Presses de l'Université de Bordeaux.

Langlade, G. (2013). Chartreuse(s) de Parme: D'une lecture subjective à l'autre. In N. Rannou (Ed.), *L'expérience du sujet lecteur: travaux en cours* (pp. 41–53). Grenoble, France: Presses de l'Université de Grenoble.

Lemieux, A. (2015). Think it through: Fostering aesthetic experiences to raise interest literature at the high school level. *Journal of the Canadian Association of Curriculum Studies, 12*(2), 66–93.

Mansoor, A. (2014). Ekphrastic practices in catalysing creative writing in undergraduate ESL classrooms. *International Journal for the Practice and Theory of Creative Writing, 11*(2), 208–227.

Many, J. E. (1991). The effects of stance and age level on children's literary responses. *Journal of Reading Behavior, 23*, 61–85.

McGee, L. M. (1992). Focus on research: Exploring the literature-based reading revolution. *Language Arts, 69*(7), 529–537.

McMahon, S. I., Raphael, T. E., & Goatley, V. J. (1995). Changing the context for classroom reading instruction: The Book Club project. In J. Brophy (Ed.), *Advances in research on teaching: Learning and teaching elementary subjects* (pp. 123–166). Greenwich, CT: JAI Press.

Ministère de l'Éducation, du Loisir et du Sport, MELS (2009). *Programme de formation de l'école québécoise, français langue d'enseignement.* 187 pages. Retrieved from: http://www.education.gouv. qc.ca/fileadmin/site_web/documents/dpse/formation_jeunes/PFEQ_FrancaisLangueEnseignement.pdf. Accessed June 28, 2017.

Moorman, H. (2006). Backing into ekphrasis: Reading and writing poetry about visual art. *English Journal, 96*(1), 46–53.

Moroye, C. M. & Uhrmacher, P. B. (2012). Standards, not standardization: Orchestrating aesthetic educational experiences. *Language Arts Journal of Michigan, 28*(1), 65–69.

National Endowment for the Arts. (2007). *To read or not to read: A question of national consequence* (Research Report #47). Washington, DC: Office of Research and Analysis.

Nussbaum, M. C. (1998). The narrative imagination. In N. C. Nussbaum, *Cultivating humanity: A classical defense of reform in liberal education* (pp. 85–112). Cambridge, MA: Harvard University Press.

Ogle, D. & Lang, L. (2011). Best practices in adolescent literacy instruction. In L. M. Morrow & L. B. Gambrell (Eds.), Best practices in literacy instruction, 4th edition (pp. 138–173). New York, NY: Guilford.

Parsons, J. & Taylor, L. (2011). *Student engagement: What do we now and what should we do?* Report conducted by the University of Alberta for University Partners, 59 pages.

Parsons, L. T. (2006). Visualizing worlds from words on a page. *Language Arts, 83*(6), 492–500.

Parsons, M. (2002). Aesthetic experience and the construction of meanings. *Journal of Aesthetic Education, 36*(2), 24–37.

Probst, R. E. (1990). Literature as exploration and the classroom tradition. In E. J. Farrell & J. R. Squire (Eds.), *Transactions with literature: A fifty-year perspective* (pp. 27–45). Urbana, IL: National Council of Teachers of English.

Purves, A. C. (1990). Can literature be rescued from reading? In E. J. Farrell & J. R. Squire (Eds.), *Transactions with literature: A fifty-year perspective* (pp. 79–93). Urbana: National Council of Teachers of English.

Purves, A. C. & Rippere, V. (1968). *Elements of writing about a literary work: A study of response to literature*. Urbana, IL: National Council of Teachers of English.

Purves, A. C., Rogers, T., & Soter, A. O. (1990). How porcupines make love II: Teaching a response-centered literature curriculum. New York & London: Longman.

Rannou, N. (2013). L'expérience du sujet lecteur: Travaux en cours. *Recherches et travaux no 83*. Grenoble: Presses de l'Université Stendhal.

Reinking, D. (2001). Multimedia and engaged reading in a digital world. In L. Verhoeven & C. Snow (Eds.). *Literacy and motivation: Reading engagement in individuals and groups* (pp. 195–221). Mahwah, NJ: Lawrence Erlbaum Associates.

Ricoeur, P. (1981). *Hermeneutics and the human sciences: Essays on language, action and interpretation* (J. Thompson trans.). Cambridge, MA: Cambridge University Press, and Paris, France: Éditions de la Maison des Sciences de l'Homme.

Rosenblatt, L. M. (1938/1976). *Literature as exploration*. New York, NY: Noble & Noble.

Rosenblatt, L. M. (1978). *The reader, the text, the poem: The transactional theory of the literary work*. Carbondale and Edwardsville: Southern Illinois University Press.

Rosenblatt, L. M. (2005/1985). Viewpoints: Transaction versus interaction—A terminological rescue operation. In L. M. Rosenblatt, *Making meaning with texts: Selected essays* (pp. 38–50). Portsmouth, NH: Heinemann.

Rouxel, A. (2012). Mutations épistémologiques et enseignement de la littérature: l'avènement du sujet lecteur. *Revista Criaçao & Critica, 9*, 1–12.

Sager Eidt, L. M. (2008). *Writing and filming the painting: Ekphrasis in literature and film*. Amsterdam, Netherlands, and New York, NY: Rodopi.

Schallert, D. L. & Reed, J. H. (1997). The pull of the text and the process of involvement in reading. *Reading engagement: Motivating readers through integrated instruction* (pp. 68–85). Newark, DE: International Reading Association.

Seel, M. (2008). On the scope of aesthetic experience. In R. Shusterman & A. Tomlin (Eds.), *Aesthetic experience* (pp. 98–105). New York & London: Routledge (Routledge Studies in Contemporary Philosophy).

Shernoff, D. J., Csikszentmihalyi, M., Schneider, B., & Shernoff, E. S. (2003). Student engagement in high school classrooms from the perspective of flow theory. *School Psychology Quarterly, 18*(2), 158–176.

Shusterman, R. (1991). Beneath interpretation. In Hiley, D. R., Bohman, J., Shusterman, R. (Eds.), *The interpretive turn: Philosophy, science, culture*. (pp. 102–128). Ithaca, NY: Cornell University Press.

Shusterman, R. (2008). Aesthetic experience: From analysis to Eros. In R. Shusterman & A. Tomlin (Eds.), *Aesthetic experience* (pp. 79–97). New York, NY: Routledge.

Sontag, S. (1966). *Against interpretation, and other essays.* New York: Farrar, Straus & Giroux.

Speigelberg, H. (1975). *Do phenomenology: Essays on and in phenomenology.* The Hague: Martinus Nijhoff.

Swanger, D. (2013). In B. White & T. Costantino (Eds.), *Aesthetics, Empathy and Education* (pp. 117–131). New York, NY: Peter Lang.

Uhrmacher, P. B. (2009). Toward a theory of aesthetic learning experiences. *Curriculum Inquiry. 39*(5), 613–636.

Wilhelm, J. D. (1997). *You gotta BE the book!* New York, NY & Urbana, IL: Columbia University Press & National Council of Teachers of English.

White, B. (1998). Aesthetigrams: Mapping aesthetic experiences. *Studies in Art Education, 39*(40), 321–335.

White, B. (2007). Aesthetic encounters: Contributions to teacher education. *International Journal of Education and the Arts, 8*(17), 1–28.

White, B. (2011). Private perceptions, public reflections: Aesthetic encounters as vehicles for shared meaning making. *International Journal of Education & the Arts, 12*(LAI 2), 1–26.

White, B. (2013). Pay attention, pay attention, pay attention. In B. White & T. Costantino (Eds.), *Aesthetics, Empathy and Education* (pp. 99–116). New York, NY: Peter Lang.

White, B. (2014). Student generated art criticism. *The Canadian Review of Art Education, 41*(1), 32–55.

White, B. & Tompkins, S. (2005). Doing aesthetics to facilitate meaning-making. *Arts and Learning Research Journal, 21*(1), 1–36.

Wiebe, S. (2013). Aesthetic/empathetic punctures through poetry. In B. White & T. Costantino (Eds.), *Aesthetics, Empathy and Education* (pp. 135–150). New York, NY: Peter Lang.

Wigfield, A. (1997). Children's motivations for reading and reading engagement. In J. T. Guthrie & A. Wigfield, *Reading engagement: Motivating readers through integrated instruction* (pp. 14–33). Newark, DE: International Reading Association.

Wigfield, A. & Guthrie, J. T. (1997). Relations of children's motivation for reading to the amount and breadth of their reading. *Journal of Educational Psychology, 89*, 420–432.

Wigfield, A., Guthrie, J. T., Perencevich, K. C., Taboada, A., Klauda, S. L., McRae, A., & Barbosa, P. (2008). Role of reading engagement in mediating effect of reading comprehension instruction on reading outcomes. *Psychology in the Schools, 45*(5), 432–445.

Wiseman, D. L., Many, J. E., & Altieri, J. (1992). Enabling complex aesthetic responses: An examination of three literary discussion approaches. In D. J. Leu & C. K. Kinzer (Eds.), *Literary research, theory, and practice: Views from many perspectives,* (41st Yearbook of the National Reading Conference) (pp. 283–290). Chicago, IL: National Reading Conference.

SECTION TWO

CHAPTER TWO

Putting Theory into Practice

Aesthetigrams: Mapping Aesthetic Experiences

BOYD WHITE

In Chapter 1 our discussion of theory was oriented largely towards students' responses to reading. In this chapter, we concentrate on interactions with visual artworks, because this is where the idea of aesthetigrams first developed. Thus, this chapter provides a little historical context and some concrete examples of students' efforts to record their encounters with artworks. To provide the historical context we begin with an article I (White) wrote in 1998. Of course, refinements in the procedure have developed over the years, so we will follow that article with a description of those refinements, a list of the categories of experiential moments to date, some more recent examples of student interactions with artworks and the dialogues they engendered.

Adapted from "Aesthetigrams: Mapping Aesthetic Experiences," first published in *Studies in Art Education*, 39(4). © 1998. Used with permission of the National Art Education Association.

Abstract: This paper describes a strategy for heightening university students' awareness within aesthetic encounters. The strategy, called aesthetigrams, is the focus of ongoing qualitative research, the purpose of which is to improve teaching and learning in regard to aesthetics-in-the-classroom A more long-term research goal is discussed briefly. It addresses the possibility for a definition of aesthetic experience to be derived from student-produced records of their encounters.

This paper describes an ongoing qualitative investigation into university-level student aesthetic encounters. I have chosen to examine the moments, or components, of the encounters and the particular manner of their interrelatedness, in order to (a) address pedagogical strategies for teaching and learning about aesthetic encounters, (b) contribute to research on the essential elements of aesthetic experience and thus to an evolving definition of the phenomenon. In this paper, I concentrate largely on a description of the first aim, although the second is implied.

The investigation is an integral part of my teaching. In a course I teach, one of my goals, for both myself and the students, is an increased understanding of aesthetic encounters. To this end, I look at documentation of student self-observation, in particular the patterns that depict their encounters. The study is a form of continuous evaluation with the intent to improve my teaching practice as it pertains to this course. My students and I are "learning how to learn" about aesthetics-in-the-classroom (Novak & Gowin, 1984). In short, the research investigates one component of my own (university) classroom practice and pedagogical problem solving. The project is small-scale and situational. The questions to be addressed emerge as the study proceeds. At the same time, I hope that my interventions will result in a significant contribution to the field of aesthetic education through the raising of questions about the nature of our experiences when we encounter art.

The study had its beginnings in a pedagogical intuition. I experimented with diagrams in the hopes of finding one that would provide a clear visual response to one of students' frequent questions: "What is aesthetic experience?" Ultimately, this led to a teaching strategy where I encourage students to find the answer for themselves, with the construction of diagrams, or maps, which I have chosen to call aesthetigrams. Like concept maps (Cliburn, 1990; Novak & Gowan, 1984; Watson, 1989), aesthetigrams strive towards a "discovery of meaning" (Cliburn, 1990, p. 212). Both depend on an ability to visualize—experiences, in the case of aesthetigrams; abstract concepts, in the case of concept maps. The strategy is quite simple, and variations on it should be adaptable to classroom teaching at several levels.

BACKGROUND

For the past few years, I have collaborated with the educational unit of a large local museum in the teaching of a university-level course designed to provide teachers, both generalists and art specialists with practical experience in aesthetically and critically oriented classroom activities to augment traditional art-making concerns. I emphasize practical educational applications in order to differentiate the course from others on campus that concentrate exclusively on examination of theory.

The practical nature of the course appears to have wide appeal. As it turns out, enrolling students have diverse academic backgrounds—music, fine arts, liberal arts, science, management as well as education. They also represent a wide range of social, cultural, and ethnic backgrounds, and include some graduates as well as undergraduates. Only a few have art or art education as their field of specialization.

The mix of students provides a pedagogical challenge—to stimulate learning appropriate to students' varied backgrounds, levels of experience and understanding of the topic. But enrolment numbers, (usually about 24 per session) do not warrant multiple sections of the course to accommodate these differing qualifications. At the same time, I like the students to work collaboratively as much as possible, in order to take advantage of the academic and cultural mix that our large urban university attracts.

The format of the course reflects these considerations. There is considerable small and large-group discussion about readings and exhibitions we attend together, and about artefacts we bring to class. The aesthetigrams, together with more traditional journal entries, provide mechanisms for "silent conversations" (Stout, 1995)—with the art and with the self, about art and the questions it raises. These silent conversations too, are ultimately shared and often challenged.

The journals are an important component of the course. We call the journals" open letters"—to emphasize the co-responsibility of student and teacher to maintain and sometimes initiate dialogue. The open letters address two slightly different tasks. The first is to depict students' encounters with art using aesthetigrams and follow-up commentary. Students must also demonstrate an understanding of the various readings, either through summaries, critiques or answers to specific questions I raise.

The second task is more flexible and personal. I encourage students to raise questions of their own on points about which they are unclear. They can also raise issues that didn't get resolved to their satisfaction in class. Commentary on any aspect of the class is also encouraged. Thus the open letters provide a lesson-by-lesson check on what the students do and don't understand, as well as what their personal concerns are in relation to the course.

RESEARCH RATIONALE

The impetus for this study was, as I stated earlier, a response to student needs, as I interpreted them. Apart from providing a mechanism whereby students can pursue an answer to the question of aesthetic experience, my concern is to have students record their encounters with art for subsequent reflection, evaluation, and sharing with others.

There are unresolved philosophical questions and advocacy issues driving the study as well. Dewey (1958) considered aesthetic experience to have an identifiable internal unity and to be an extension of everyday experience. Beardsley (1958) largely adopted Dewey' position.

Beardsley's (1969) Presidential Address to the American Society for Aesthetics is part of an extended debate between himself and Dickie (1964, 1966, 1971) as to the very existence of aesthetic experiences. Dickie argued against the notion of an aesthetic attitude and insisted that unity is not a generalizable feature of aesthetic experiences. Dickie (1974) also took exception to Beardsley's insistence on the presence of affect in aesthetic experiences. If Dickie is right, then Efland (1990), who claimed that art is concerned primarily with feeling and imagination, was wrong (p. 263); and those of us who concur with Efland and Beardsley may have been leading our students astray.

On the issue of advocacy, there have been certain historical influences in the relatively recent past. For instance, aesthetics was one of the four sub-disciplines of Discipline-Based-Art-Education (DBAE) (Smith, 1989b), which became a major focus in art education in the 1980s. (The other three sub-disciplines were: studio practice, art history and art criticism). One strong advocate of the emphasis on aesthetics was Vincent Lanier (1987), and more recently, Paul Duncum (2007). Others, such as David Best (1984, 1996), Jan Jagodzinski (1981), and more recently, Kevin Tavin (2007), have regarded the focus on aesthetics to be a misguided, probably elitist focus. Could both sides be right?

In short, it would appear that there was, in those years, sufficient disagreement among aestheticians and educators, not to mention student puzzlement, to warrant another look at the question expressed by my own students. (Today, in 2016, the discussion continues). Dickie (1974) observed that "... the complete range of aesthetic experience has to be examined before a general conclusion may be drawn" (pp. 18–19). I do not claim that the work of my students covers Dickie's "complete range," but I believe it may add a worthwhile component to the growing body of educationally oriented research on the topic (Csikszenthmihalyi & Robinson, 1990; Housen, 1983; Parsons, 1986, 1987a, 1987b; Weltzl-Fairchild, 1991). The work described in this paper is an incremental step in that direction.

THEORETICAL UNDERPINNING

I take the position that perception underlies meaning-making and that art education, in one form or another, is about meanings and the values we attach to them, based on perceptual experiences. This is largely a phenomenologically oriented bias, or at least the part of phenomenology that makes perception a fundamental primary source of experience and subsequent learning. As Husserl (1977) noted:

Most of the things in our life-world ... are immediately experienced by us as mentally significant things; they are not seen as merely physical, but in their sensuously experienced shape ... a two-sided material-mental object ... stands before our eyes. (p. 84)

This statement need not be taken as incontrovertible fact. What it does, however, is provide one perspective for investigation of the phenomenon in question, namely aesthetic encounters. In other words, I may pose the statement as questions. For example: What is the nature of an aesthetic encounter? If it has an immediacy, what is the significance of that quality?

With reference to this latter question, Spader (1994) noted that our customary acknowledgement of day-to-day phenomena is akin to an immediate "gestalt-grasp" (p. 175). He also made the point, however, that there are limitations to the depth of knowledge available through such quick categorizations, especially where a complex phenomenon is concerned. "[Alternatively] To know all of the essential elements ... is to see more than we saw when all we had was a grasp of the as-yet-undifferentiated total essence of the phenomenon." (Spader, 1994, p. 175)

This is similar to Richmond's (1988) argument in regard to aesthetic understanding. He stated," Having an understanding of something entails having a picture of how its parts are organized into some kind of whole or pattern" (p. 54). Richmond continued: "... to understand ... [a phenomenon] ... will be to distinguish and relate its parts." (p. 54) He also made the point that a full understanding is dependent upon such distinction making being done with an awareness of the wider context in which the phenomenon exists. "Thus, objects [or events] as meaningful patterns of parts and relationships are understood against a background of ideas, values, theories, events, assumptions, practices, etc., that provide their context." (p. 54)

My diagrammatic strategies address Spader's and Richmond's concerns. The aesthetigrams draw attention to the individual elements, or phenomenological "moments" of aesthetic encounters, and encourage an accompanying awareness of the context, or "aesthetic field" of which they are a part (Berleant, 1970). If successful, the aesthetigrams should also graphically demonstrate meanings, even if these are difficult to capture in a few words. What follows is an elaboration on that possibility.

THE PROCESS

With all due respect to the problematic nature of assumptions, it seems safe to say that each aesthetic encounter requires a participant (viewer) and an object or event to be viewed, and that each occasion takes place within a certain context of time, location, social conditions, and so forth. To initiate my students' investigations I encourage them to account for these three emphases, that is, (a) viewer,

(b) object, and (c) context. Thus, if my students find that their initial responses are largely confined to social issues, formalist concerns, or self-absorption it is easy enough to show them the limitations of such a stance. For example, in an extreme case of contextual focus, one student, on being asked for her responses to a Dutch Baroque painting, talked almost exclusively about the history of privilege, the power of money and church, and so forth. There was no acknowledgement of her opinion of the work or feelings in relation to it, although these were certainly implied. And there was no mention at all of the actual imagery, the manner of painting, indeed, no reference to any physical presence of the work. Awareness that other factors can enter into the experience is often enough to encourage students in successive experiences to stretch their mental horizons, so as to encompass more of their potential aesthetic fields. Readings such as Parsons (1986, 1987a, 1987b) also draw attention to the potential breadth of aesthetic fields; and his descriptions of the professional critics, Henry and Hugo, provide ideal models.

Of course, my students have not reached the sophistication of Henry and Hugo. So, to encourage students in that direction, which I interpret as aware-ness of the part to be played by the viewer/object/context categories, I encourage explicit noting of what they are experiencing. For, with clear evidence of experi-ence-as-experienced, they can reflect on the viewer/object/context categorization and address, next time, possibilities they may have missed at first.

To help students articulate their encounters I provide suggestions for 13 cat-egories of experience in a list of "Possible Experiential Moments." Most of the 13 experiences are, in turn, broken down into a number of sub-categories. Together they provide over 50 possible response considerations. The list is compiled from a number of sources (Housen, 1983; Lankford, 1984; Smith, 1989a; Weltzl-Fairchild, 1991), among others, and perhaps most importantly, from comments from the students themselves.

I emphasize that the list is provisional. It is not intended to be definitive or to dictate the nature of anyone's encounter. It simply provides a vocabulary for moments that students may recognize, but which they might otherwise not have noticed. The challenge for students is to be aware of the range of their experiences, to record them accurately, and not to be pre-selective of supposedly appropriate responses. Any number of readings, such as Feldman (1987), Feinstein (1989), Anderson (1988), Lankford (1984), and related discussions, may prompt an initial viewing. One of my goals, however, is to develop student self-confidence to the point where they may choose whatever method or combination of methods seems appropriate or they may disregard the proffered models altogether in favour of their own intuited approaches. Naturally, as students extend their readings and experience, their intuitions tend to incorporate the acquired learning.

Regardless of which approach to the encounter they deliberately adopt, to begin the search for meaning students write down the content and sequence of their experiences in some form of private notation. Students generally seem comfortable with the idea of writing about their encounters. There are no stipulations about the format of the writing, only that it should be completed as soon as possible after the encounter, or even during, if they don't find the act of writing to be intrusive on the main activity. The list of "Categories of Possible Experiential Moments" is there to support their initial observations. Some students use the list to check off categories of experience during the encounter. Subsequently they translate their initial, brief records of a specific encounter into the aesthetigram format and follow this with a written commentary. These commentaries give students a chance to elaborate on what might otherwise remain cryptic and to refine their thinking on the encounter. For example, students sometimes realize there was an added component to their experience that they had at first overlooked. They only realize this upon reflection on their aesthetigram-in-progress. The realization is often prompted by the requirement for the written explanation (and therefore, extended examination of the aesthetigram). Word and image work in concert in the quest for meaning.

The aesthetigram thus becomes a form of outline for a critique—one firmly grounded in experience. The critiques perform three functions. First, they provide me with another form of documentation to compare with the aesthetigrams. Second, they provide an opportunity for students to convert experiences into reflections and to hone their communication skills. Finally, they provide a focus for collaborative evaluations that students perform on each other's observations. There is a constant demand for a showing of evidence to back up one's statements in regard to the work in question. If students are successful their critiques are persuasive.

STUDENT EXAMPLES

Aesthetigram 1, below, is a typical example done early in the course by a student with no previous background in formal art instruction. I show it to demonstrate a neophyte's capability for involvement in aesthetic encounters, her ability to capture both what she did and didn't see, and the aesthetigram's potential for initiation of dialogue among the student, her peers, and myself.

The work that the student chose to describe is a large, non-objective painting (approximately eight feet wide by ten feet high) *Mutation Serielle Vert-Rouge*, by Guido Molinari (1966). The painting consists of a series of 18 vertical stripes of equal width, each about five inches wide. The colours range from vivid green and orange to muted earth tones. The composition consists of a pattern on nine colours, repeated twice. Despite the size of the work and the few design elements involved, the repetition is not immediately apparent.

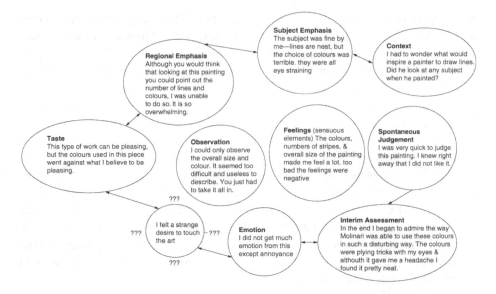

Fig 2.1. Aesthetigram 1.

From: *Studies in Art Education*, 39 (4) (Summer, 1998), p. 327.

In the above diagram (Aesthetigram 1), the size of the circles corresponds to the degree of impact, that is, the more noticeable the moment, the larger the circle. I suggest to students that probably four sizes of circle will suffice for most encounters. I also suggest that they use the alphabet to indicate the sequence of events. In this example, the student either forgot this latter directive or felt it was beyond her powers of observation at that time.

The three largest circles in the centre are slightly overlapped. Not only were those moments of equal impact but simultaneous as well. Because this student did not indicate a sequence of experiences, it is difficult to know at what point her awareness of TASTE took place. What is apparent in the commentary, however, is that it was immediately present in her initial SPONTANEOUS JUDGEMENT as well as in her SUBJECT EMPHASIS, her FEELINGS and EMOTION moments. While she does acknowledge the moment of TASTE, she obviously felt that it was not as dominant a moment as most others. That is, only two other circles are of equal size to TASTE, indicating the relatively low level of impact, as perceived at that time. It was necessary for the student to see just how influential her taste was before she could, in effect, put it on the agenda in a subsequent viewing. My task was simply to point out to her what she had herself indicated in regard to the interrelations of the various moments. In other words, while she does indicate an awareness of some interconnections, at the time when she made this aesthetigram she had not seen the wider implications.

What is also missing from this aesthetigram is some sense of how the student arrived at her INTERIM ASSESSMENTS, which are reservedly positive, in contrast to the negative experiences that preceded this later stage. In other words, there must have been at least one other interim moment such as an EMOTION that combined her declared annoyance with something rather more accepting. Awareness of the necessity that such a moment must have taken place would only become apparent to the student upon reflection on her aesthetigram, with a little judicious questioning on my part to encourage the reflective process.

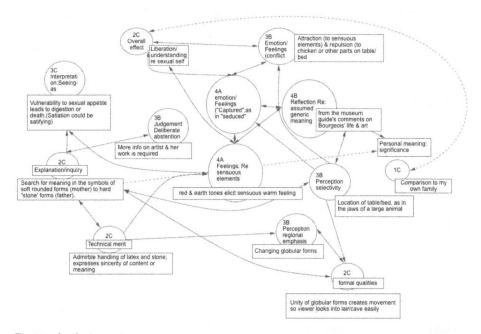

Fig 2.2. Aesthetigram 2.
From: *Studies in Art Education*, Vol. 39, No. 4 (Summer, 1998), p. 329.

Aesthetigram 2 is from another student a little further along in the course. This aesthetigram is based on an installation titled *Destruction of the Father* (1974) by Louise Bourgeois. The work has a lair-like setting, approximately 7 feet wide by 6 feet deep by 5 feet high. It consists of an assemblage of beach ball-sized rock shapes (made out of latex), some of which hang from the ceiling, like mammalian-shaped stalactites; others sit on the floor. These surround a small, bed-like platform from which smaller stones and other vaguely animalistic forms have been carved. The neutral, earthen colours of the materials are suffused with red lighting, which gives the whole installation a glowing quality, like a bank of votive candles in a church.

In comparison with our first example, this student made somewhat more distinctions (number of itemized moments) in relation to the work and the links are more fully explored. She was able to indicate the sequence of actions, alphabetically. The student also designated to each circle a numerical value, from 1 to 4 that corresponds to the size she allocated to each. So it is easy to see not only when the moment took place, relative to the others, but also the degree of impact she felt it had on her.

A number of the student's observations are worth noting. As in the first example, this student acknowledges the spontaneous impact of feelings in relation to the work. In this case, however, her FEELINGS: SENSUOUS ELEMENTS circle merely implies a connection with perception. She doesn't specify it. Even in her follow-up notes "description" emerges largely as a reflection of her affective response to the various components of the work. This is not to say that the student is satisfied with a "gestalt-grasp" of the occasion. Indeed her "C" step involved a detailed looking at materials, formal considerations, and so forth. These remain, however, less important for this student than more contextually inspired interpretations notable in her SEEING AS or PERCEPTION: SELECTIVITY circles. The student does acknowledge some very personal connections, such as may be seen in her OVERALL EFFECT and PERSONAL MEANING circles; but these are decidedly not dominant moments. In other words, the student is conscious of the input from her personal life but this is balanced against what are to her at least as important contextual and formal considerations. Thus, the student is a pretty close fit to the ideal I described earlier in terms of her ability to balance the three competing emphases within an aesthetic encounter, that is, viewer self-awareness, the context surrounding the event, and the physical nature of the artwork itself.

Two "Possible Experiential Moments" are notable by their absence. The first is "bracketing." While such a moment does not appear in the aesthetigram, the student does make explicit reference to it in her accompanying notes. Certainly, the concept was important to her, as the following quotation makes clear:

> How did I initially miss the table/bed in the center with its stone phallic and rounded objects, some in the shape of chicken legs, giving a morphogenetic feel to the cave? The initial seduction was becoming a repulsion, so I "bracketed" the initial seduction response for further investigation, especially on becoming aware that others, too, were finding the idea of devouring your father as disgusting.

I believe the omission from the student's aesthetigram may be due to the fact that I had neglected to make specific reference to bracketing in the list of "Possible Experiential Moments." We altered the list during that session.

The other moment that does not appear in the above aesthetigram, except as a deliberate abstention, has to do with judgements. The student does clearly indicate the abstention, however, and in her notes she elaborates on her reasons.

These are characterized by a cautiousness, an awareness that her background in contemporary art is limited, and that definitive judgements require a level of expertise that she has not attained. This stance is followed some paragraphs after by a statement that, on the surface, is about feelings, but is nonetheless a form of judgement. She says,

> My feelings were both of repulsion to this perversity and admiration for the strength of character in Louise Bourgeois to be able to transcend these negative feelings into a positive expression—an act or work of exorcism for herself and others. ... Why was I so impressed ...? I had to distance myself from the act of viewing her work, to reflect on my re-ignited values about art making and the art world and how it relates to my own.

In these lines, it is apparent that feelings, values and judgement become intertwined. But this was not clear to her until she began to elaborate on her aesthetigram. It is arguable that the student's choice of work to critique is a form of implied judgement, and perhaps this should be acknowledged. What is also clear is that the student felt she was engaged in significant learning. She speaks of her realization that she has a preference for works that are initially gratifying because of their sensuous qualities and technical merit, but that ultimately she enjoys the emergence of multiple meanings that are the result of the synthesis of moments. For her the evolving meanings and values provide the lasting, overall effect. I find parallels in the comments of other students, such as: "I often wonder if my attraction to these works of art which deal with elements of creation and birth are related to a stage I am going through in my life ..."

The student observations are significant because they demonstrate awareness that each individual moment is recognizable as having a correspondence with other facets of one's life experiences. Students feel the connections between old and new experiences, and this synthesis is the basis of their learning. It is also important to note that the student aesthetic encounters do not show evidence of an altogether different breed of experience. The individual moments are part of the continuum of daily life, as Dewey (1958) insisted, and it is precisely this attachment to the lifeworld that enables aesthetic encounters to provide meaning and significance and to reflect our values, and as I have argued elsewhere (1993), our values are reflected in our feelings.

The following quotation from a student, and virtually all of the aesthetigrams I have examined, would seem to contradict Dickie's insistence that feelings don't necessarily play a part in aesthetic encounters." With the second viewing I changed my mind, but perhaps more importantly I changed my feelings ... I realize my original viewing was primarily analytical ..." My observation that feeling is virtually always present applies as long as feeling is defined as Langer (1957) intends, that is, as anything that can be felt, rather than too narrowly as in Dickie's emotion-oriented definition.

On the other hand, contrary to Parsons's (1986) assertion, the aesthetigrams suggest that emotion is not always a factor in aesthetic encounters. Some possible explanations for the non-appearance of emotion come to mind. One is that although the students thought they were having aesthetic encounters, they were not. A full exploration of this possibility would have, as an initial requirement, a definition of aesthetic experience with which we could all agree. While this paper hints at a movement in that direction, we are not there yet.

A related possibility to explain the occasional absence of emotion is that, as one reviewer noted, the requirement to do an aesthetigram may inhibit emotional responses, due to the emphasis on analysis. In other words, the task of understanding their responses may have got in the way of more unfettered, genuinely aesthetic ones. I, too, have been concerned with this possibility. To minimize it I try to build student confidence in their abilities to respond before I add the aesthetigram requirement. We also spend considerable time discussing the generally affective nature of our responses. Still, I also emphasize that they record only what they experience; and not all students record emotion.

In short, art education does not have generally agreed upon parameters for aesthetic experience. Nor is the research sufficient to allow us to insist on the inclusion or exclusion of particular elements of experience such as emotion. In this study, however, I have been more concerned with student learning.

The students' written commentary and aesthetigrams are products of their active and enthusiastic participation in their own learning. This varies from student to student, of course, and some are more successful than others. The course puts a premium on a student's ability not only to observe objects as fully and accurately as possible, but to be self-aware as well. This includes an awareness of the context surrounding the event. The encounters and corresponding aesthetigrams and critiques necessitate a tolerance for working towards what is to a large extent an unknown entity. There is no single correct answer; and this characteristic is problematic for a few students. Finally, the work demands a willingness to experiment, both with one's own responses and in the creation of the aesthetigrams, as well as a certain facility with language. One's personality enters into the equation to some extent, as does one's speaking and writing ability. Nevertheless, to my recollection only one student failed to produce any aesthetigrams. That student was atypical in several respects. The majority of students comment in their open letters on the usefulness of aesthetigrams to their learning, as exemplified by the following excerpt:

> … Looking back over my aesthetigrams I am pleased to see the pictorial evidence of the complexity of responding to art. It is interesting that critiquing has involved such a constant interplay of feeling, intellectual analysis and reflection …

Just as our everyday life experiences and the associations we make to previous ones are frequently unpredictable, so too the aesthetigrams demonstrate a certain unpredictability. The contributing components do not appear in a consistent order of experience. This suggests that there is no hierarchy of experiences within aesthetic encounters, at least not one that is generalizable across the student population I have dealt with so far.

SUMMARY

I have shown how aesthetigrams not only express students' encounters with art, as each understands it at that moment, but also how the aesthetigrams provide the basis for continued examination and questioning—both by the student and by me as the teacher. That is, they provide a useful point of reference for student/teacher interaction, as well as an evidential source for the study of individual components that may ultimately provide us with a working definition of aesthetic experience. My initial study of aesthetigrams, combined with accompanying documentation, commentary and final assignment (an extended critique based on one or more aesthetigrams), tentatively confirms Richmond's and Spader's assertions that pattern awareness leads to increased understanding of phenomena. It is my hope that others will find aesthetigrams an intriguing site from which to launch further research and widen the dialogue.

REFERENCES

Anderson, T. (1988). A structure for pedagogical art criticism. *Studies in Art Education, 38*(1), 28–38.

Beardsley, M. (1958). *Aesthetics problems in the philosophy of criticism.* New York: Harcourt, Brace & World.

Beardsley, M. (1969). Aesthetic experienced regained. *The Journal of Aesthetics and Art Criticism, 28*(1), 3–11.

Berleant, A. (1970). *The aesthetic field: A phenomenology of aesthetic experience.* Springfield, IL: Charles C. Thomas.

Best, D. (1984). The dangers of "aesthetic education." *Oxford Review of Education1, 1*(1), 159–168.

Best, D. (1996). Values in the arts. In J. M. Halstead& M. J. Taylor (Eds.) *Values in education and education in values* (pp. 79–91). London: Falmer Press.

Cliburn, J. W. (1990, February). Concept maps to promote meaningful learning. *JCST*, 212–217.

Csikszenthmihalyi, N. & Robinson, R. (1990). *The art of seeing: An interpretation of the aesthetic encounter.* Malibu, CA: J. Paul Getty Museum and The Getty Center for Education in the Arts.

Dewey, J. (1958). *Art as experience (16th ed.).* New York: Capricorn Books.

Dickie, G. (1964). Myth of the aesthetic attitude. *American Philosophical Quarterly, 1*(1), 56–66.

Dickie, G. (1966). Attitude and object: Aldrich on the aesthetic. *The Journal of Aesthetics and Art Criticism, 25*(1), 89–91.

Dickie, G. (1971). *Aesthetics: An introduction.* New York: Pegasus.

Dickie, G. (1974). Beardsley's theory of aesthetic experience. *Journal of Aesthetic Education, 8*(2), 13–23.

Duncum, P. (2007). Reasons for the continuing use of an aesthetic discourse in art education. *Art Education, 60*(2), 46–50.

Efland, A. (1990). *A history of art education: Intellectual and social currents in teaching the visual arts.* New York and London: Teachers College Press, Columbia University.

Feinstein, H. (1989). The art response guide: How to read art for meaning, a primer for art criticism. *Art Education, 42*(3), 43–53.

Feldman, E. (1987). *Varieties of visual experience* (3rd ed.). New York: Abrams.

Housen, A. (1983). *The eye of the beholder: Measuring aesthetic development.* Unpublished doctoral dissertation, Harvard University, Cambridge, MA.

Husserl, E. (1977). *Phenomenological psychology: Lectures, summer semester, 1925* (John Scanlon, Trans.). The Hague: Martinus Nijhoff.

Jagodzinski, J. (1981). Aesthetic education reconsidered: Or please don't have an aesthetic experience. *Art Education, 34*(3), 26–29.

Langer, S. (1957). Expressiveness. In *Problems of art: Ten philosophical lectures.* (pp. 13–26). New York: Charles Scribner's Sons.

Lanier, V. (1987). A*R*T, a friendly alternative to D. B. A. E. *Art Education, 40*(5), 46–52.

Lankford, L. E. (1984). A phenomenological methodology for art criticism. *Studies in Art Education, 25*(3), 151–158.

Novak, J. D. & Gowin, D. B. (1984). *Learning how to learn.* Cambridge: Cambridge University Press.

Parsons, M. J. (1986). The place of a cognitive approach to aesthetic response. *Journal of Aesthetic Education, 20*(4), 107–111.

Parsons, M. J. (1987a). *How we understand art: A cognitive developmental account of aesthetic experience.* New York: Cambridge University Press.

Parsons, M. J. (1987b). Talk about a painting: A cognitive developmental analysis. *Journal of Aesthetic Education, 21*(1), 37–55.

Richmond, S. (1988). Aesthetic education: Metaphor and the understanding of works of art. *Canadian Review of Art Education: Research and Issues, 15*(2), 53–67.

Smith, R. (1989a). *The sense of art: A study in aesthetic education.* New York/London: Routledge.

Smith, R. (1989b). *Discipline-based art education.* Urbana: University of Illinois Press.

Spader, P. H. (1994). Phenomenology and the claiming of essential knowledge. *Husserl Studies, 11*, 169–199.

Stout, C. J. (1995). Critical conversations about art: A description of higher-order thinking generated through the study of art criticism. *Studies in Art Education, 36*(3), 170–188.

Tavin, K. (2007). Eyes wide shut: The use and uselessness of the discourse of aesthetics in art education. *Art Education, 60*(2), 40–45.

Watson, G. R. (1989). What is … concept mapping? *Medical Teacher, 11*(3/4), 265–269.

Weltzl-Fairchild, A. (1991). Describing aesthetic experience: Creating a model. *Canadian Journal of Education, 16*(3), 267–280.

White, B. (1993). Aesthetic judgments as a basis for value judgments. *Canadian Review of Art Education: Research and Issues, 20*(2), 99–115.

Note: I have made some changes to the routine since those first classes. In Chapter 4, we provide the current list of "categories of possible experiential moments" and discuss more recent developments in the strategy.

CHAPTER THREE

More Recent Developments

Visual Art

BOYD WHITE

"All real living is meeting."

—Martin Buber, *I and Thou*

As I hinted at the beginning of Chapter 2, I have made some changes to the routine since that article was first published. This chapter, therefore, will begin with a brief comment on a slight change in notation of aesthetigrams. Then I will introduce the most recent version of the list of categories for possible experiential moments. I have found that students have also benefitted from a strategy offered by R. L. Jones Jr. (1979), so I include an explanation of that strategy as well. The chapter concludes with a more recent example of one participant's interactions with artworks and the dialogues they engendered.

AESTHETIGRAM NOTATION CHANGES

At some point, as students became more adventurous and ambitious in their individual artwork encounters, I realized that it is conceivable that a person might have more than 26 sequential moments to record. In that case, the alphabet would be insufficient. So in more recent aesthetigrams most participants use numbers to indicate sequence. Then too, on the hard copy printout that I give to students, where I list the possible categories of experiences, I continue to propose acknowledging a range of i–iv to indicate relative impact, as a preparatory step in the construction of an aesthetigram. But on the aesthetigram itself, it is often easy to indicate the nature of that impact by simply varying the size of the shape (usually ovals) that the student uses to depict that moment. Then, too, computer software is more sophisticated today than it was in 1998. So I recommend colour coding of the various categories. This makes it easy to see what the predominant categories are within any single encounter.

EXPERIENTIAL MOMENTS

Preamble

Below, we provide a list of categories of possible experiential moments. The list has grown somewhat over the years as students suggest categories and subcategories that were not previously listed, but that they experienced. So the list should be regarded as a work in progress. It is also important to stress that it would be virtually impossible for an individual to incorporate all categories into one aesthetigram. For example, if a student were to acknowledge that her familiarity with art history dominated her response, then she would be unlikely to also note a frustration with a lack of such knowledge, which is a subcategory within the "knowledge/content" general category. So the list is intended to offer suggestions as to how to categorize individual moments of experience. It is not meant to be a compulsory shopping list.

Finally, the point of allocating individual moments into categories is that the categories suggest patterns of response behaviour. Once a student is aware of her patterns then she is able to decide whether to broaden her range of considerations and how she might go about doing that. For example, in the 1998 article, in Chapter 2, I described one student whose involvement with an artwork was restricted to contextual considerations. Upon realizing that, she had the option to examine other considerations—the physicality of the work, her affective responses to it, and so forth.

Categories of Possible Experiential Moments

Initial Explanatory Note

Below, the two short lines on the left, under each suggested moment, are for, on the left line, the designation of the sequence, and on the right hand line, the relative impact of the moment, for example, in **1 iv** the **1** would mean that this was the first moment in the sequence; the **iv** would mean that, on a scale of i–iv, this was a very pronounced, rocked-back-on-one's-heels moment. An **i** would be a barely perceptible moment on the periphery of one's consciousness.

The VCO (viewer/context/object) box is there to help people think about the direction or inclinations of their responses and the emerging patterns. It provides a reminder as to the main orientation of the moment; for example, a strong viewer-oriented moment would require the "v" box to be pencilled in. A moment that acknowledges some shared orientation could result in one or more boxes being partially filled in. Ideally, at least over time, a viewer's responses would be evenly divided across all three foci, with the aim of arriving at a balance between moments. Of course, artworks tend to elicit responses in keeping with the questions they ask. For example, a highly conceptual piece with no representational subject matter is likely to elicit an intellectually based "object" focus. If the viewer feels that she is being made to feel inadequate in her grasp of the work and its context, she may also be "viewer" oriented in that respect. On the other hand, if a work evokes strong personal memories, then the "viewer" box is likely to predominate that occasion. So I ask participants to pencil in the boxes to the extent they feel appropriate to the occasion.

The "sequence" and "impact" lines, together with the "vco" box serve as a guide to construction of the aesthetigram.

Perception:
Rating

— —	[v | c | o]	I Observation: A looking without particular aim or emphasis; a detached visual tour of the artwork.
— —	[v | c | o]	II Description: A tendency to itemize or identify features of the work. This may be further subdivided into: Selectivity—
— —	[v | c | o]	(a) Local Emphasis, i.e., based on the phenomenally objective field—number of colours, shapes, specific items, etc. And/Or
— —	[v | c | o]	(b) Subjective Emphasis, e.g., personally favourite colour, topic, etc.
— —	[v | c | o]	III Regional Emphasis or Generalization of Form—a tendency to synthesize, i.e., to assemble the parts into a whole. E.g., two dots side by side, with one in the middle beneath them begin to suggest a face.
— —	[v | c | o]	IV Other considerations?
Feelings re:		(You do not need to have a precise word to define your feeling, just a sense that this is where your attention is focused.)

— — | v | c | o | I Sensuous Elements: i.e., the affective quality of colour, line, balance, pattern—any visible content

— — | v | c | o | II Technical Merits, i.e., how influenced are you by the technical virtuosity, or lack of it?

— — | v | c | o | III Generic Expressive Significance—here, your assumption is that others will interpret the image as you do, or should do so.

— — | v | c | o | IV Subjective Expressive Significance—here, you acknowledge an idiosyncratic response for:

— — | v | c | o | (a) a particular colour or topic, etc.

Or

— — | v | c | o | (b) an overall feeling regardless of your inability to pinpoint the cause(s) or to attach a precise label to the feeling.

— — | v | c | o | V Other considerations?

Emotion:

— — | v | c | o | I A sub-category of **Feelings**, those to which a single precise term may be attached, e.g., happy, sad, embarrassment, anger, etc.
Or

— — | v | c | o | II A sub-category of **Feelings** to which a combination of terms may be attached, such as attraction *and* repulsion, anger *and* admiration, etc.

— — | v | c | o | III Other considerations?

Attitude

— — | v | c | o | I Positive

— — | v | c | o | II Negative

— — | v | c | o | III Indifferent

Taste:

— — | v | c | o | I A general, or habitual, preference for certain types of imagery, topics, styles, etc. over others.

— — | v | c | o | II A random preference—can be an arbitrary choice particular to this image.

— — | v | c | o | III   Other considerations?

Memory:

— — | v | c | o | I   Associations to previous occasions in your life, connected to art, e.g., biography of the artist, anecdotes, schools of painting—<u>not specifically comparative</u>.

— — | v | c | o | II   Associations to artworks, actual locations, occasions, etc.—i.e., specifically comparative. (See also: **Comparison**)

— — | v | c | o | III   Associations <u>not</u> connected to art, e.g., religious ideologies, political stances, personal reminiscence, or recollection.

— — | v | c | o | IV   Other considerations?

Daydreams/Reverie:

— — | v | c | o | Not quite memories; more an empathic state of imaginative reverie induced by the encounter, a kind of becoming one with the work.

Seeing As:

— — | v | c | o | I   An imagining of the object as a metaphor. E.g., VanGogh's *Sunflowers* as a symbol of the Christian soul; essentially a comparative act between what is presented and what it represents to you.
Or

— — | v | c | o | III   Other considerations?

Interpretation:

— — | v | c | o | I   An exploration of the meaning of the work. E.g., is the distant ship in Gericault's *Raft of the Medussa* sailing towards or away from the raft?

Comparison:

— — | v | c | o | Ii   A comparison between the work and some other artwork, object, or event.

— — | v | c | o | Ii   A comparison between the work now and on some other occasion

Expectations:

— — | v | c | o | I   An imagining of the object/event beforehand—essentially a comparative act between what you anticipate and what you have encountered before. I.e., an object-oriented expectation.
Or

— — | v | c | o | II   An anticipation of your response to the object/event, i.e., a self-oriented expectation.

— — | v | c | o | III   Other considerations?

Explanation/Inquiry:

— — | v | c | o | I   You treat the image like a puzzle or symbol(s) to be decoded or problem to be resolved—essentially a positive reaction.

— — | v | c | o | II   Your dominant sense is one of puzzlement, lack of access to the "secret"—essentially a negative reaction.

— — | v | c | o | III   Hesitancy, typified by «I'm not sure». This is a positive response rather than a negative one, showing a willingness to consider options. It could also be considered to be a postponement of judgement.

— — | v | c | o | IV   Other considerations?

Reflection re: i.e., deliberate critical activity, a questioning of:

— — | v | c | o | I   The overall affective nature of the work.

— — | v | c | o | II   Specific content

— — | v | c | o | III   Individual Formal Quality(ies)—line, balance, pattern, etc.
Formal Analysis (formal synthesis)

— — | v | c | o |

— — | v | c | o | IV   Technical Merits, i.e., how important are they?

— — | v | c | o | V   Assumed Generic Meaning

— — | v | c | o | VI   Personal Meaning/Significance, a private context
And/Or

— — | v | c | o | VII   In relation to the artist's society (context)

And/Or

| v | c | o | VIII | In relation to your own society (context)

| v | c | o | IX | Other considerations?

Reflection that leads to Bracketing

| v | c | o | I | Awareness of the need to momentarily put aside a particular idea or feeling, in respect to any or all of the three categories (viewer, context, object) in order not to impede further open-minded investigation.

Knowledge/Content — Intellectual stances:-

| v | c | o | I | Does your knowledge of art history, biology, biography, for example, dominate your response?
Or

| v | c | o | II | Does your awareness of a lack of contextual knowledge frustrate your attempts at interaction with the work?

| v | c | o | III | Other considerations?

Judgment:

| v | c | o | I | Initial, spontaneous response.

| v | c | o | II | Interim assessments—a questioning or verification of initial response, or a change of mind, perhaps a gradual evolution.

| v | c | o | III | Tentative closure assessment.

| v | c | o | IV | Adamant closure assessment.

| v | c | o | V | Deliberate abstention from judgement.

Additional Moments:

| v | c | o | For example, a temporary "blank" or rest.

| v | c | o | A tendency to involve other senses.

| v | c | o | Associations to (seeing as), e.g., "black as hell," "heavenly."

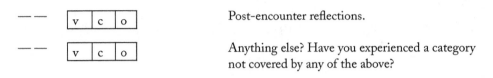

Post-encounter reflections.

Anything else? Have you experienced a category not covered by any of the above?

In addition to the "vco" boxes in the above list, I have also found a diagram by R. L. Jones Jr. (1979, p. 98), Figure 1, below, to be very useful. The intent of Jones's diagram is similar to that in my viewer-context-object differentiation, insofar as he sees the individual moments in encounters with artworks as being possible to allocate to various foci, which in his case he represents by quadrants in a circle, as in the diagram below.

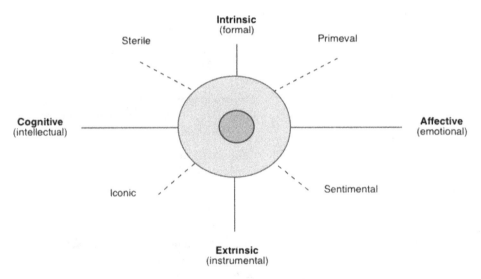

Fig 3.1. Jones's Diagram (Adapted from the 1979 *Studies* article).

EXPLANATION OF JONES'S DIAGRAM

Jones (1979) argues that a truly "aesthetic" response is achieved only once a number of experiential moments are in equilibrium, or "balanced." The diagram above indicates the categories of moments to which Jones refers. According to this model, it is apparent that aesthetic response could be characterized by attention to an intellectual/emotional interaction. Jones's model also indicates the potential richness and complexity of a response. That is, his model represents possibilities for considerations of those moments that radiate away from affect or cognition.

The vertical and horizontal axes suggest contending theoretical orientations. Thus, the intrinsic pole represents a concentration on form for itself alone, focus on a particular colour for its "fit" in the overall design, for example. At the other extreme is the extrinsic orientation in which the work is considered for its instrumental, or use-value alone. This could range from a concern that a painting match the décor of one's living room, to insistence that artworks must promote social justice or raise other ethical questions.

The cognitive pole represents a purely intellectual stance in relation to the work. Exclusive attention to historical or contextual data would exemplify this orientation. Its opposite, the affective, represents a purely emotional response.

In between these vertical and horizontal poles are their diagonal affiliations. Thus, the "sentimental" extreme represents a combination of affect and instrumentality, for example, a wallowing in grief or indulging in pleasure for its own sake. Its opposite, the sterile, is a combination of intellectual and formal concerns. A painter, musician, or writer who wants to grasp another's technique would occupy this category.

The other diagonal addresses the two remaining quadrants. As Jones notes, "The primeval is a type of non-aesthetic response similar to the sentimental, but its focus is on the emotional rather than the extrinsic." (p. 101) Themes such as birth, death, mother, father, hero, and so forth, such as Carl Jung explored in his study of archetypes, and to which we may have instinctive responses, would be examples in this quadrant.

Finally, its opposite, the iconic, combines an intellectual with an instrumentalist orientation. As Jones suggests, an interpretation of the work purely in terms of symbol systems, such as found on Canadian west coast totem poles, or popular culture clothing logos, would exemplify this emphasis.

Exclusive attention to any one of these categories would represent an extreme and non-aesthetic response. To become aesthetic, the experience would have to move from the periphery of the circle towards the centre, that is, to become less extreme, and to combine with or work in conjunction (find a phenomenological balance) with the other considerations.

Further, while the affective side of the circle suggests the possibility for spontaneous responses, the intellectual side suggests the possibility for sustained reflection. This is an important consideration because it indicates that an aesthetic response is virtually impossible to achieve in the few seconds that are commonly devoted to viewing artworks as people stroll, rather quickly, through museum galleries. People can make spontaneous judgements based on emotional responses or knowledge—recognition that an artwork is representative of the Baroque period, which they happen to like, for example—but that does not qualify as a full encounter, and would not lead to new insights. In short, full aesthetic responses require sustained effort and attention over a time dictated by one's energy and interest.

Thus, I often advise my students, after they have done an initial aesthetigram or two, to rearrange their observed moments to where they think those moments fit on Jones's grid. In the next section, I will show an example of a student's attempt to do just that.

DIALOGUES WITH MARY

Mary (pseudonym) was one of eight people who volunteered to participate in a small group exercise in a local museum a few years ago. The participants were all classmates in a graduate class in art education in a neighbouring university. The instructor, my colleague, gave them the option to participate in my exercise as part of their requirements for the course. Mary had a background in studio art, more specifically, figurative sculpture. So Mary was not typical of the undergraduate, non-specialist pre-service teachers with whom I regularly have contact. I was interested to see what difference her studio art background and more advanced stage of studies would contribute to the exercise. Given the constraints of text length, I could not include the work of all the participants here. I chose Mary's work because it reflected well the work of her fellow participants, was clearly described, and was of a convenient length.

Unlike my usual undergraduate classes where I suggest themes and have students choose a work from within one of them, in this case Mary was free to choose any work from the museum collection. Figures 3.2 and 3.3 show the piece she chose by Clifford Rainey, as exhibited in the Montreal Museum of Fine Arts. What follows are Mary's three aesthetigrams (visual maps) and commentary, my subsequent comments to Mary, and reflections on the exercise.

Preliminary note: I altered Mary's aesthetigram slightly in order to fit the format of this text. For example, normally the size of the ovals is sufficient to indicate the impact of the moment. But the length of some of the category words, such as "reflection" (J), necessitated using a slightly larger form than she would otherwise have used, considering that this particular moment was apparently of only slight impact (i). Then too, some of her moments had more impact than the size of the ovals suggests, due to lack of space. So the impact is recorded here in terms of the italicized roman numerals—$i - iv$. Normally I have participants use roman numerals to differentiate "impact" from "sequence" numbers. But Mary used the alphabet to indicate the sequence, so I have kept that although I find numbering easier to follow. I did not change any of her observations. Most of Mary's observations are included in the rectangles beside the corresponding ovals.

Fig 3.2. Clifford Rainey (Born in Whitehead, Northern Ireland, in 1948).
Lightness of Being
From the series "Freedom of Conscience," 1990.
Cast glass, plate glass, laminated glass, various materials.
185.4 × 27.9 × 24.1 cm Acquisition # 2007.210.1–3.

Fig 3.3. The Montreal Museum of Fine Arts, Gift, Anna and Joe Mendel Collection.
Photo MMFA, Christine Guest.

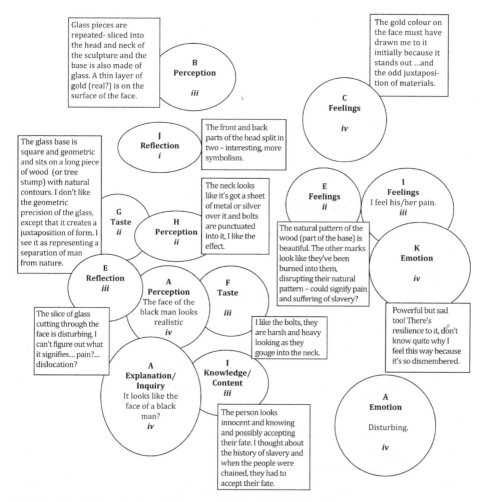

Glass pieces are repeated- sliced into the head and neck of the sculpture and the base is also made of glass. A thin layer of gold (real?) is on the surface of the face.

B
Perception
iii

The gold colour on the face must have drawn me to it initially because it stands out ...and the odd juxtaposition of materials.

C
Feelings
iv

J
Reflection
i

The front and back parts of the head split in two – interesting, more symbolism.

The glass base is square and geometric and sits on a long piece of wood (or tree stump) with natural contours. I don't like the geometric precision of the glass, except that it creates a juxtaposition of form. I see it as representing a separation of man from nature.

G
Taste
ii

H
Perception
ii

The neck looks like it's got a sheet of metal or silver over it and bolts are punctuated into it, I like the effect.

E
Feelings
ii

I
Feelings
I feel his/her pain.
iii

The natural pattern of the wood (part of the base) is beautiful. The other marks look like they've been burned into them, disrupting their natural pattern – could signify pain and suffering of slavery?

K
Emotion
iv

E
Reflection
iii

A
Perception
The face of the black man looks realistic
iv

F
Taste
iii

The slice of glass cutting through the face is disturbing, I can't figure out what it signifies... pain?.... dislocation?

I like the bolts, they are harsh and heavy looking as they gouge into the neck.

Powerful but sad too! There's resilience to it, don't know quite why I feel this way because it's so dismembered.

A
Explanation/
Inquiry
It looks like the face of a black man?
iv

I
Knowledge/
Content
iii

The person looks innocent and knowing and possibly accepting their fate. I thought about the history of slavery and when the people were chained, they had to accept their fate.

A
Emotion

Disturbing.

iv

Fig 3.4. Mary's 1ˢᵗ aesthetigram (Mary created, March 18, 2016).

MARY'S COMMENTARY, MARCH 18

My first aesthetigram is based on a sculpture that I saw at the Montreal Museum of Fine Arts called "Lightness of Being" by the artist Clifford Rainey. The artwork is actually part of a series that the artist did called "Freedom of Consciousness." When I first noticed it, I was interested in it *because* it looked like the *sculptured head of a black person (I am of mixed race, both black and white)*. I am *also interested in figurative sculpture* and I studied it in my studio art classes *many years ago*. For me though, *I'm always interested in what contemporary artists do* with the human figure, and *this was definitely a contemporary artwork*. Specifically, what struck me about the piece was that *it wasn't a regular head* in the formal sense with all of its features intact, but was *a bit dismembered* or disfigured. The *irregularity* of it drew me to it because *I was curious* as to what it was about. The sculptor Rainey, whom I had never heard of before up until this point, chose to put a piece of *flat glass horizontally above the nose* area of the head and also had *two similar pieces in the neck* area. I thought this was *visually interesting but disturbing,* which was *my initial response* in the aesthetigram map, and *I couldn't quite figure out if I liked it or not.* But *I chose the piece for a challenge too. I didn't want to examine my responses to a familiar artwork* because *there's no fun in that.*

My first two initial responses (indicated by the letter "A") had a big impact on me (indicated by *iv*) which included finding the piece disturbing and then identifying it as realistic and looking like a black man.

[Actually, Mary cited three initial moments—in the perception, explanation, and emotion categories. But because she chose to put the "emotion" one off to the right hand side, she apparently forgot about it. Since her "A"s indicate that she had those moments simultaneously, her map would have been more coherent if she had moved the "emotion" circle to underneath, but overlapping, the explanation/inquiry oval.]

I don't mean to say that it looked disturbing because of who I thought it looked like but because it was a disfigured-looking head made out of glass. The latter observation was part of simultaneous experiential moments that came right after my initial responses. Another feature that was apparent was a *thin layer of gold paint (or the real thing, I'm not sure?)* over a part of the face. Also, between the two sheets of glass that cut into the neck was a sheet of metal covering a portion of the neck area with nuts and bolts fastened in it. *All of these features,* a glass head, cut at different places with sheets of glass slipped through it, gold painted on a portion of the face, and bolts piercing through the neck, suggested to me that the piece *had to be about slavery.* Of course, *I wasn't really sure.* I remember *questioning myself* why I hadn't made the connection of the colour of the gold on the figure's face to the trade of gold with the commercialization of slavery right away, because *I remember at first just seeing a colour and then making the connection after.*

Under the category "Knowledge/Content" I made reference to *my knowledge* about the history of slavery but much later from my initial responses. This was at "I" which was near the end of my viewing time (which ended at "K") The reason for this, as I mentioned earlier, was because *I wasn't sure* if I was making the right references so I needed to spend time with the piece and to really see it. This is actually what made this research experience interesting for me, the fact that *I actually was able to understand my capacity for understanding the artwork as I was viewing it.* It is like my understanding of the sculpture, or *deepening awareness of it,* came in little waves. And *this happened again* when I was able to label it sequentially in the aesthetigram map. I found this interesting.

The fact that there was the *possibility* of the sculpture's content dealing with slavery made it more compelling for me to view it as well. *I'm forever happy to see artists deal with the latter theme because I think it's a story that needs to be retold over and over again.* Oddly enough, I found it interesting that the artist who made this piece was from *Northern Ireland* (and I found out he'll be speaking at the museum in May as well).

Since I was so focused on the head, it was later in the viewing, from letter "E" and on, that *I began to notice the base, or bases,* since it had a few. The sculpture head was on a square clear glass base (made up of sheets of glass layered one on top of each other) and then this was on a long piece of natural wood (or tree stump) about 4-feet high or so. *I thought this was odd,* it was more mixing of different materials that didn't really fit together. I mentioned the latter in "G" designated saying also, that though *I didn't like* the precision and sterile quality of the glass base as it sat on the wood base, it created this *tension* that was *strange* but it *aesthetically worked* somehow. All of this happened *because* I spent more time than I would normally spend viewing one piece. To make the kind of connection with the piece that I did, normally that would happen over a few viewings of the same piece and on occasion, in one viewing. But, particularly a piece like *Lightness of Being* with its mixed materials of glass and wood, organic shapes and geometric shapes, and its disfigured head with sheets of glass going through it, these *normally make it hard viewing for me,* even though I've seen a lot of art. I probably go to museums or galleries more than the average person who has other interests but not nearly as much as some practicing artists or art critics do. That being said, no matter who you are, *you are going to have your preferences* when it comes to what you like and don't like. What I like to do then, when I go see work at museums or galleries (and with this research project) is to *question my preferences* and really *try and "see"*—as opposed to "look at" art work that at first or second glance I may dismiss. It's amazing what you notice when you give it time. This is what I found happened with this sculpture head that I saw. I chose something that I felt drawn towards, though I was not quite sure if I liked it. *I've come to really like it* and will do my second aesthetigram on this piece (though it will have to be from an image) because the exhibit was shut down just recently.

MY RESPONSE TO MARY'S FIRST AESTHETIGRAM

Mary, as you see, I've highlighted a number of words or phrases in your text. [In this publication, the highlights have been converted to italics]. These all correspond to what I think could be assigned into various categories—some of them, above and beyond what you indicated in your aesthetigram. Your aesthetigram, by the way, is a fine beginning, clear and easy to follow. I think you could probably dispense with the numbers because you have indicated the degree of impact with the size of your circles. (I know the model you have followed comes from your reading of my article. I've tried to simplify the routine somewhat since then. Now I recommend just varying the circle size and using numbers to indicate the sequence.)

[As I have just noted above, the italicized numbers help in this case].

So, back to your text. I'll pick out just a few of the highlighted comments so you get the idea. For example, Let's start with "because". The word suggests a certain contextual influence that you then go on to explain. It's important because it establishes one framework of your viewing "bias". There are others, of course, for example, your art background being another.

In reference to your decision not to revisit a more familiar work for this exercise, you state: "there's no fun in that." This implies your enjoyment of challenge and willingness to explore the unfamiliar—a most welcome quality to bring to such an exercise. I appreciate it.

Later in your text you comment on the fact that you like to see artists' works that remind us of the evils of slavery. I'd like to see that represented somehow in your aesthetigram too. But we can delve further. You mention being of both black and white heritage. How significant is that fact for you?, that is, positive, negative, insignificant, etc. I ask because our cultural roots do often influence how we interpret our worlds.

Then you mention your interests a number of times. These are contextual moments as well as viewer-oriented ones. Of course you also have numerous "regional" perceptions where you focus on specific details of the sculpture, as in B. In D you use a regional focus while at the same time becoming aware of certain feelings.

[The phrase "regional focus" was an error on my part. What I should have listed was "local" focus because Mary was actually noting details at this point rather than the whole "region" of the work].

A phrase you used more than once is "I wasn't sure". Good! This is a variation on an inquiry category. Maybe we should add a hesitancy category.

[I have since added that subcategory].

I won't go through all the rest. I'm sure you get the idea. I'm trying to tease out the layers of meaning making influences. I look forward to your next submission.

[Upon reviewing Mary's aesthetigram I noticed something that I missed initially. That is, Mary has two "I" moments—"feelings" (on the right side of her map) and "knowledge/content" (at the bottom of the map). The letter designation implies that these were simultaneous, or co-intended, moments. As such, the map would have been clearer if those ovals had been placed side-by-side or overlapping. But perhaps Mary was already

anticipating a grouping of categories, since her "feeling" moments are all in the same area of her map. Grouping of categories becomes evident in her second aesthetigram.]

MARY'S FOLLOW-UP NOTE

Saturday, March 20
Hi Boyd,

Here is my 2nd aesthetigram and text, I hope it's complete. Please let me know if you need changes.

Also, one question (it may be a stupid one?):

If we do the aesthetigram first and write the text version after, do you want us (or can we) to alter the aesthetigram map?

Here are some revisions for aesthetigram #1 that you can change if you feel it's necessary:

These are the answers regarding your comments (and that I didn't include in my aesthetigram that may have some relevance to your research)

1. Regarding the contextual influence related to the sentence: "because it looked like the head of a black person"—**this would have been an impact of 4.**
   – I am of mixed race so seeing some head of a sculpture that looked to me of someone of colour drew me to it. I was interested in seeing what the artist may have been trying to express using this subject.
2. Re: the contextual influence "that I am from both black and white heritage"
   – it would be a **"positive" and significant impact (and/or an impact of 4).**
3. Re: the contextual influence "that I'm interested in figurative sculpture (and this is was a part of my studio training)—**this would be an impact of 4.**
4. Re: the contextual influence that "it's important that the story of slavery be told over and over again"—**would be an impact of 4.**
   Again, feel free to change my aesthetigram to fit the above in!

MARY'S ACCOMPANYING COMMENTARY, MARCH 20, 2016

My second aesthetigram is based on a photo image of the sculpture that I saw at the Montreal Museum of Fine Arts. Unfortunately, the exhibit that the sculpture was a part of was shut down before I could go view it a second time. The curator was kind

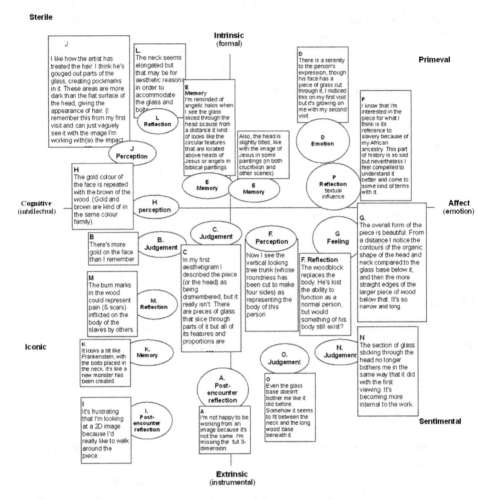

Sterile

Intrinsic (formal)

Primeval

J

I like how the artist has treated the hair. I think he's gouged out parts of the glass, creating pockmarks in it. These areas are more dark than the flat surface of the head, giving the appearance of hair. (I remember this from my first visit and can just vaguely see it with the image I'm working with (so the impact

L.

The neck seems elongated but that may be for aesthetic reasons in order to accommodate the glass and bolt.

L. Reflection

J Perception

E Memory

I'm reminded of angelic halos when I see the glass sliced through the head because from a distance it kind of looks like the circular features that are located above heads of Jesus or angels in biblical paintings

Also, the head is slightly tilted, like with the image of Jesus in some paintings (in both crucifixion and other scenes)

D

There is a serenity to the person's expression, though his face has a piece of glass cut through it. I noticed this on my first visit but it's growing on me with my second visit.

D Emotion

P

I know that I'm interested in the piece for what I think is its reference to slavery because of my African ancestry. This part of history is so sad but nevertheless I feel compelled to understand it better and come to some kind of terms with it.

H

The gold colour of the face is repeated with the brown of the wood. (Gold and brown are kind of in the same colour family).

H perception

E Memory

E Memory

P Reflection textual influence

Cognitive (intellectual)

Affect (emotion)

B

There's more gold on the face than I remember

B. Judgement

C. Judgement

C

In my first aesthetigram I described the piece (or the head) as being dismembered, but it really isn't. There are pieces of glass that slice through parts of it but all of its features and proportions are ----

F. Perception

F

Now I see the vertical looking tree trunk (whose roundness has been cut to make four sides) as representing the body of this person

G Feeling

F. Reflection

The woodblock replaces the body. He's lost the ability to function as a normal person, but would something of his body still exist?

G.

The overall form of the piece is beautiful. From a distance I notice the contours of the organic shape of the head and neck compared to the glass base below it, and then the more straight edges of the larger piece of wood below that. It's so narrow and long

M

The burn marks in the wood could represent pain (& scars) inflicted on the body of the slaves by others.

M. Reflection

Iconic

K

It looks a bit like Frankenstein, with the bolts placed in the neck. It's like a new monster has been created.

K. Memory

O. Judgement

N. Judgement

N

The section of glass sticking through the head no longer bothers me in the same way that it did with the first viewing. It's becoming more internal to the work.

Sentimental

I

It's frustrating that I'm looking at a 2D image because I'd really like to walk around the piece.

I. Post-encounter reflection

A. Post-encounter reflection

A

I'm not happy to be working from an image because it's not the same. I'm missing the full 3-dimension.

O

Even the glass base doesn't bother me like it did before. Somehow it seems to fit between the neck and the long wood base beneath it.

Extrinsic (instrumental)

Fig 3.5. Mary's second aesthetigram (Mary created, March 20, 2016).

enough to send an image of it through email and that is what I was working from. I have yet to find out about the artist's intentions of his sculpture and will include that with my last visual responses to it. However, I did try to find images of the sculpture on the Internet (to find something better than I currently have to work with) but couldn't find any, which makes me wonder if I'll find any specific information about the piece at all—we'll see. Concerning my first response in this aesthetigram ("A" with an impact of *iv*) and also in my 9th response ("I" with an impact of *iii*), I mention that the viewing effect was not the same, since with sculpture you really need to walk around the piece to get a full impression of it. Nevertheless, it was possible for me to work from the photo and the memory of my first visit, especially since *I really like the piece.*

I made a realization upon writing this text about my "interim assessment" response "C" of the sculpture head being "dismembered," which had a sizeable impact (*iii*) on me. In my last aesthetigram, I wrote about the latter experience and used the harsh description of the piece looking dismembered. Alternately, in the current aesthetigram, I made reference that all of the features of the head were intact and it was only a piece of glass horizontally slicing through the nose and eye areas that caused me to describe it so harshly. When I began to write this report, I realized that it does in fact deserve harsh terminology if it does at all relate to issues related to slavery (or any severe and difficult situations for that matter). In retrospect then, I think that my judgment in "C" about its surface details was probably connected to my emotional response in "D" (with a high impact of *iv*) and judgment response in "N" (with an impact of *iii*). The former response included me feeling that the piece was "growing on me" and I felt it had a "serene" quality because of the expression on the face. The latter reaction included the fact that I no longer was bothered by the piece of glass sliced through the face of the person. What I think happened (or is happening) is that *the more I see the piece, the more I appreciate it on an aesthetic level but this doesn't mean it has to cancel out the relevance of its somber meaning (if it does mean what I think it does)*. So, I questioned my use of the word "dismembered" and its validity for description, though its use was justified. I realize that *the beauty of art is its ability to be paradoxical*.

Another aspect about my reaction to the sculpture that I found interesting was about my simultaneous "memory" responses in "E" which had a big impact on me (*iv* and *iii*, respectively) and which may have been related to my "feeling" response ("G" with an impact of *iv*). The glass slice through the head of the sculpture reminded me (in the first "E" memory response) of halos that you see around biblical figures *like Jesus or angels in religious paintings* and some sculpture. Also, *the head is slightly on a tilt* which I recalled (in the simultaneous "E" response) were *similar to the angle of the heads of some people depicted in religious paintings* (as in crucifixion and other scenes). I also commented on the overall form and beauty of the entire piece in "G" (including its bases), which helped me to notice the tilted head even more. At first, I thought that citing this biblical reference was kind of absurd but remembered that all responses count. One could assume then, that if the artist's intention for the sculpture was to be about slavery, then this black person could, in a sense, have been *"crucified"* just by being a victim of slavery. Similarly, staying with the latter theme, in my "Reflection" response in "P" that had a high impact of *iv*, I said that I was interested in the art piece because of the topic of slavery (or my assumption that it was about this). The latter was based on a contextual moment because of my own African ancestry, which I think creates a heavy bias in terms of my choice and interpretation of some art works.

I continued to make references about the sculpture concerning its meaning, as happened with my simultaneous responses in "F" (each having an impact of *iii*), "K" (with an impact of 2), and "M" (with an impact of *iii*). With the former responses, at first I noticed that the long wood base could perhaps symbolize the person's actual body. Whereas, in my first aesthetigram responses regarding the wood, I saw it more as an abstract representation where the burn marks on it could possibly signify pain and suffering. Also, in terms of the wood juxtaposed next to the glass base, I viewed it as suggesting a separation of man from nature. I think all of these references could have relevance to the artwork's overall meaning, but just to say that in my second viewing experience, I began to see the piece in more concrete terms. Similarly, I go on to say ("F") that the wood base could represent whatever is left of a body. Regarding the burn marks in the wood ("M"), I make the same "regional" perceptions about it as I did in my first aesthetigram – that they could represent the pain and suffering endured during slavery.

[Again, Mary is referring to specific burn marks, which makes them a local focus as opposed to a regional one. I have since corrected that directive in the list of experiential moments.]

Lastly, I do make a low impact (*i*) response about the subject looking like Frankenstein, which is related to a "memory" association to my film experiences watching the movie, a lot as a child. Perhaps it could have been given a higher impact, maybe a *ii* or *iii*? I hesitate to change it because at the moment of viewing I can't remember if, when I made the reference, it impacted me strongly or not? I vaguely remember thinking that it was a silly reference but again, I thought I better include it. In retrospect too, the idea that this figure could be like a Frankenstein made me think that it's not a crazy reference to slavery if viewed abstractly, in terms of thinking of it as a *monstrous set of circumstances* that were unleashed.

Lastly, I had more viewing moments related to the surface quality of the sculpture that included "regional" and "subjective" perceptions, a reflection about "technical merit" and another "interim assessment." My response related to perception ("J" with an impact of *iii*) is in response to the artist's treatment of the hair on the head of the sculpture, which isn't an interim assessment because I didn't mention it in my last viewing response; however, I do remember noticing it (maybe this counts?). With the perceptual response "H" (with an impact of *iii*) I made a connection with the repeated use of the colour brown and gold being similar in the colour family sense (if you add yellow—and maybe some orange and white—to brown you will get a gold colour). Concerning a viewing moment dealing with the artist's technical merit ("L" with an impact of *i*), I noticed that the neck of the piece seemed elongated and considered this to be for aesthetic reasons. The artist may have done the latter in order to make them more noticeable and to further convey his intended meaning. With my "interim assessment" response ("B" with an impact of *iii*), I noticed that there was more gold on the face of the head than what I remembered in my first visit.

I am looking forward to my third viewing and think that the text version will be much shorter than this one, mainly because I think I've done a bulk of the looking or seeing now. But then again, I could be wrong!

MY RESPONSE TO MARY'S 2ND AESTHETIGRAM

As with Mary's first commentary, I highlighted a few lines to help me with my responses. But not all my comments were prompted by highlighting. For example: [In reference to moments A and I in paragraph 1] I note that you categorize these as postencounter reflections; but isn't this a new (2nd) encounter? So, actually they are comparison moments, between what you remember of your first visit and the current moment.

In response to the highlighted statement, "I really like the piece": Since this is a strong response, surely it belongs on your aesthetigram.

On your aesthetigram you mention that the head isn't actually dismembered—an indication that you are honing your perceptions. Nonetheless, your "harsh" (your term) terminology remains; i.e. your judgement hasn't changed. So your heightened perceptions justify/reinforce your initial judgement.

[In reference to the first highlighted comments at the bottom of paragraph 2]: Right! Aesthetic involvement doesn't deny intellectual contributions. Actually, we should probably discuss what you mean by "aesthetic level". I'm assuming you mean more than an appreciation of form.

[In reference to the second highlight, paragraph 2, regarding the paradoxical nature of artistic beauty]: Interesting. Did this thought come to you during the encounter? (We're in your 2nd paragraph after all.) Or was it more of a post-encounter reflection?

[In reference to Mary's comparisons between the glass in the sculpture and religious halos]: Good comparisons.

[In reference to "all responses count"]: Right!

[In reference to Mary's use of the verb "crucified"]: Good metaphor. This then becomes a "seeing as" moment.

[In reference to Mary's comment about her African ancestry and her bias]: Yes, I think it is important to acknowledge this part of yourself in your meaning making.

[In reference to Mary's slight change in interpretation between the two visits to the work, paragraph 4]: So do you reject that interpretation now, or could the base represent both body and suffering?

[In reference to Mary stating that she now sees the work "in more concrete terms"]: Less symbolically? [A sentence later, Mary reinforces the idea that the burn marks could symbolize pain and suffering]: OK, you've answered my question above.

[In reference to Mary's Frankenstein statement being perhaps a "silly comment"]: We can't help the thoughts and feelings we have; they are part of who we are, our history too.

[In reference to Mary's phrase: "monstrous set of circumstances"]: Again, a good metaphor, a "seeing as" moment.

[In reference to Mary's question regarding whether what she noticed initially, but didn't comment on at the time, counts]: It all counts.

[In reference to the last word in Mary's commentary]: I didn't intend to highlight the word "wrong" but that's how this "track changes" program works. I just want to add a couple of words. First, as you've no doubt noticed, your second aesthetigram is much more detailed than the first. Also, your moments appear to be balanced between the four quadrants. You might want to try a simplified version of your aesthetigram, using circles just big enough for your letters, and omitting all the details, just to see how you would distribute your moments, that is, some closer to the centre than others, some clustered close together? At any rate, this is a good step. At the conclusion of your third encounter I'm hoping that your text will provide a form of critique of the work, based on your experiences of it—a kind of summation of your meaning making in relation to this work. One last thing: Could you send me the image too? It will help me in my reading of your interpretations.

See you tomorrow evening.

P. S. I didn't change anything on your first aesthetigram. You've obviously considered those points now in your second visit. It's good to see the evolution.

SOME FURTHER THOUGHTS ON MARY'S SECOND AESTHETIGRAM

In Mary's second aesthetigram, she made an effort to locate her encounter moments within Jones's quadrants. And as I mentioned above, those moments seem to be reasonably balanced between the four quadrants. Some of those placements, however, are questionable. Her post-encounter moments A and I, for example, would seem to fit more on the Affect side of the diagram—"It's frustrating"; "I'm not happy." Then too, moment H, a discussion about colour, is arguably more Sterile than strictly Cognitive. I wonder too about moment G. Mary's comment about beauty would seem to place that moment more in the intrinsic quadrant. These are debatable points, however, and Mary could probably have defended her choices if I had raised the positioning question at the time. But I didn't. I was pleased to see the thought and effort Mary put into the exercise.

MARY'S THIRD COMMENTARY

First I'll describe how to read my third aesthetigram in terms of where I've placed my experiential moments and their impacts onto Jones' four quadrants. The largest dark blue coloured circles with white letters represent the high impact moments,

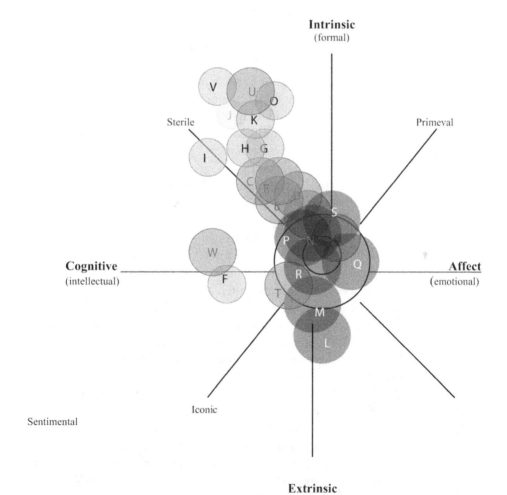

Fig 3.6. Mary's third aesthetigram. (Mary created, April 12, 2016).

or 4, the second largest lighter blue circles with red letters represent an impact of 3, the smaller circles that are sky blue with black letters stand for an impact of 2, while the smallest circles with grey lettering stand for an impact of one. I've mainly put my high impact moments closer to the centre of Jones' quadrant because I felt that these moments were close to what he would call an aesthetic encounter, or where the formal, intellectual, emotional and instrumental moments merged into one. I don't necessarily think that a high impact moment has to directly translate into an authentic aesthetic moment, as with "U" which is quite far from the centre between the formal and sterile categories, and a moment that had an impact of 3 and corresponded to my questioning still, whether the gold on the face was real or just paint. Similarly, another post-encounter moment with an impact of three that didn't fall into Jones' centre was "W," which is off to the left of the centre and relates to the cognitive quadrant. The latter moment corresponded to when I found out about the brief description about the sculpture written by the artist (I will talk more about that later). As I said though, many of my high impact moments (even three with an impact of 3) fell into the category of authentic aesthetic encounters. For instance, my first high impact moments of 4 were "L" and "M," where the former represented my experiential moment where I noticed that they had moved the piece to the very front entrance of the glass exhibit (which was larger this time around), where before it was placed in a back corner and back section of it. The latter moment represented my noticing how the lights on the ceiling hit the face of the sculpture, reflecting its gold and making it shine in a really striking manner. I initially rated both moments as an "object-oriented expectation" and compared them to what I anticipated versus what I had encountered before within a contextual orientation, since they related to the space of the exhibition. For me, noticing the sculpture in the new location and the vibrancy of its shining face had something to do with its use value, in the sense of drawing in the audience (possibly from the perspective of the curator?), and its formal aspects, which the shiny face is part of. As well, because I felt the overall effect of the sculpture was quite striking, there were also emotional elements involved (and possibly a cognitive component because I had to think about the moments on some level—I hope this isn't stretching it). So, because the moments fit into these 3 (maybe 4) areas, I placed them near the centre of Jones' quadrant.

The second point, which is important to mention, is that this viewing experience allowed me to see the actual sculpture (versus the photo I worked from last time) because it had been re-installed into the glass exhibit at the Montreal Museum of Fine Arts for the up-coming larger show this May (represented as "R"). Seeing the work in its actual three-dimensional form was better than seeing it in the form of an image. Moving chronologically in order of my experiential moments, it seems that my first six were perceptual responses relating to regional emphases such as the larger size of pock marks or holes around the entire head ("A" with an impact of 3), areas of the face are pushed in creating angular grooves and one area on the left side of the face has a large hole in it ("B with an impact of 3), the glass splices in the head and neck area are not round, as I thought, but broken and non-geometric ("C" with an impact of 3), the wood tree stump base is flat at the front and the rest is rounded in its natural state along its edges ("D" with an impact of 3), the bolts in the neck are really rusty ("E" with an impact of 3), and the eyes of the figure look a little oriental, though the rest of the features look very much like that of a black person ("F" with an impact of 2). I imagine I reflected on the surface details of the piece because it was my way of getting drawn into the piece once again, after not seeing it in its three-dimensional form for some time. For the next three moments (two were simultaneous) I made judgments questioning my responses in my last aesthe-tigram. The first was "G" which had a relatively high impact of three and included me thinking that the distortions on the face (areas where it was pushed in—see "A") affected its look of serenity, but only if you noticed them, if you didn't, the face still looked serene. The simultaneous moment was perceptual with a regional emphasis with a lower impact of 2 and included noticing that the chin area also had grooves and were pressed in at certain areas ("G"). The next judgment was "H" with a low impact of 2, where I noted that the gold colour of the face was more vibrant and covering a larger area of the face than I had noticed before (but this could have been because of the new source of light shining on it).

My next moment was a reflection concerning the sculpture's more formal aspects in which I was concerned with the back part of the head and neck area that was quite straight compared to being more at an angle as with the usual form of a head and neck ("I" with an impact of 2). I wondered if the artist had intended to do this and also if he had worked from a live model or not? The next two moments are perceptual again, and based on the surface qualities. The first is "J" with the lowest impact of 1 in which I simply note that the geometric glass base right under the head sculpture is made up of eight sections fused together. The next moment "K" with an impact of 2, is where I noticed that the glass piece cutting through the head also lodged through the ears as well, something I hadn't noticed during the first and second viewings. I'm skipping "L" and "M" since I mentioned them ear-lier. "N" fell into the category of taste, even though it was about its surface qualities and had a high impact of 4 on me. The latter moment included my really loving the repetition of the colour brown throughout the whole piece, as in the gold of the face, the rusty bolts, the brown wood, and if you can stretch your imagina-tion, the colour of the black man that the piece was intended to replicate (I will mention more about this later). "O" was a low impact of 2 where I noticed more surface qualities again, like the long cracks in wooden base of the sculpture.

With the experiential moment "P" with an impact of 4, I was drawn to wonder what the artist's intentions were about making this sculpture. This brings me to my post-encounter experiential moment "W," where, after obtaining a description of the piece from the museum's archives, I was happy to know that the piece represented a black man and I was on the right track! However, the latter is all that the description revealed to me and mentioned nothing else. The description reads "Sculpture sitting on a glass pedestal representing the head of a black man with a golden face, cut horizontally by layers of glass." So much for knowing more about the artist's intentions about his work, I guess it will always be a mystery. Despite not really knowing the artist's meaning, for me, I feel confident that my instincts were correct and it surely must be about slavery. Since I want to complete my last five experiential moments, I'll briefly discuss them before returning to the meaning I made of this sculpture. Continuing with "Q" (since I mentioned "R" in paragraph 2) that had an impact of 4, I made an assessment regarding my being struck by the sculpture's beauty and how much I really loved it. The latter is an evolution from my previous two aesthetigrams, where the piece seems to be growing on me, or at least remains at this level of appreciation based on Jones' definition of aesthetics. "S" is based on perception again (impact of 4), where because the whole piece is standing on a pedestal (about 30 cm high) and you must look up at it (instead of at eye level as before), it gives it a more monumental feeling. I put the latter circle on the aesthetigram near the centre between the formal and primeval categories, since for me this experience was about the totality of the formal aspects combined, while it also recalled a kind of archetype of a memorial tribute to something grand or important. "T" (with an impact of 3) was an "additional moment" placed near the centre and related to my wishing that I could buy the piece (along with some other pieces in the show) because of their beauty. This often happens when I go see work that I like but in the end I go home empty handed! The reflection "U" (impact of 3) has me still wondering if the gold on the face is paint or the real thing, while the last perceptual moment is "V" (impact of 2) where I notice that the neck area is also distorted (like the face) and is pushed in and irregular on some parts of its surface areas.

At this point, I will summarize the meaning I have made of Clifford Rainey's sculpture with respect to my experiences of his work. In terms of constructing meaning from my third viewing of the sculpture, I didn't really seem to make any, except to question what the artist had in mind for it (see "P"). I think I had exhausted my reservoir for trying to make sense of the piece in my first and second aesthetigrams. I guess I was also expecting to understand a little more about the piece from information gleaned from outside sources. The latter proved not to be the case as first, there was no information about the specific piece I chose on the Internet, and second, when I got the very brief description about Rainey's work from the archives department of the museum, it said very little about the work other than it being "the head of a black man." So, at the moment, I am left with my own personal meaning I have made of the work, which I am confident has to do with slavery. I initially seemed to have been drawn to the artist's sculpture and had a series of contextual moments that related to both my cultural background and my interest and background in art (which I didn't record in my first aesthetigram but wrote about in the text). In terms of my background, which includes African ancestry, I chose the piece because I first noticed that it was (and is) the head of a black man. I was curious to know more about it, especially since I felt it could be related to the theme of slavery. For instance, it had gold colour on the face, bolts attached to its neck, glass pieces sliced through it, and a long wood base, which all denoted a relationship to slavery for me, at first, more on a subconscious level. For me, the gold colour of the face represented the trading of gold for slaves, the bolts signified where the shackles and chains held them in place, the glass was more symbolic and indicated pain, dislocation, and a transparency of the whole situation in the 21st century (or the 20th century since the piece was made in 1990) and the story of its people being told more readily, and the wood seemed to represent nature, while its juxtaposition with the glass seemed to indicate a fragmented sense of it. I experienced all of the above and described it in my first aesthetigram. As well, I took an interest in the piece because of my background in making figurative sculpture. In the second aesthetigram, I continued to elaborate on making meaning from the sculpture and took issue with the glass slice through the head, which is very apparent. I found symbolism with the latter material to religious iconography, specifically to the halos seen around Jesus or angels in religious paintings. With reference to the Jesus symbol, I elaborated and connected the representation of the slave as a figure that had been in a sense "crucified" too. Similarly, I made references to the burn marks on the wood base that could signify the slave's body as significations of pain and suffering. I also made reference to early Frankenstein films that I saw when I was a child and how the work reminded me of it because of the bolts in the neck area. The latter could be a metaphor for the horror (the monster) of the commercialization of slavery that was unleashed in the 16th century. Regarding the third aesthetigram, there was really no meaning making at all as I mentioned earlier, except for wondering what the artist's intention was. This was most likely because I felt like I made all the assumptions I could about it and also felt on some level that "I got it." Instead, I made a lot of perceptual observations based on the surface details, some judgments regarding what I thought/felt about the piece, as well as some reflections about its formal qualities and two object-oriented expectations regarding its new location in the exhibit and how the piece was affected by this. I had a post-encounter moment regarding the information I received about the artist's description of his work, which only helped me to know that it was intended to be a head of a black man. As I said earlier, from the latter I feel that I can deduce the rest of the meaning of the piece (realizing too that it may not be entirely correct). Other than that I found the exercise interesting and revealing in terms of how it allowed me to see the evolution of my thinking, feeling and meaning making with respect to an artwork.

Mary

MY COMMENTS TO MARY REGARDING HER THIRD ENCOUNTER

A helpful conclusion. Just a couple of brief comments: You mention that there was "no meaning making at all". I think what you have in mind is no "new" meaning—because all of your experiences of the work up until this point, and the meanings derived from those experiences, don't just disappear. If you think of each encounter with the artwork, and your daily life that surrounds such encounters, as consisting of individual layers of meaning, like some geological formation, they layer up, provide the sediment for future experiences. That is, how you experience encounters with other artworks in the future will be influenced by your encounters—your meaning making—with the Rainey piece.

The other point I think worth addressing is your acknowledgement that the meaning you derived from the work "may not be entirely correct." It would be more appropriate to say that your interpretation today is not necessarily the entire story. Your continuing life experiences will influence future interactions with Rainey's or others' artworks, and meanings will alter accordingly.

I'm pleased that you found the exercise worthwhile. You confirm my conviction that making and commenting on aesthetigrams helps participants gain a better understanding of patterns of meaning making. Your observations are thorough and your examples will be very useful to show others. I would be interested to hear if you find, as I expect, that the exercise influences your future interactions with artworks. Keep in touch.

Best wishes,
Boyd

FURTHER THOUGHTS ON MARY'S INTERACTIONS WITH RAINEY'S WORK

I began this section by stating that I wanted to see what differences there might be in capacities for aesthetic response and development between my generalist undergraduate pre-service teachers and a graduate student with a background in studio art and art education. Their common ground, of course, is that aesthetigram exercise is new to all my participants. As such, it tends to level the playing field in terms of how to map and discuss their individual moments. All aesthetigrams are unique, even non-replicable, in some respects because there is no template that must be followed. And no two people respond to an artwork in precisely the same way. So, differences between one and another are to be expected.

Mary had an advantage over those without an art background in terms of the confidence and agency with which she approached the assignment. This was evident in her willingness to tackle a work with which she was not familiar. And that lack of familiarity placed her on a level similar to that of my more neophyte participants. But Mary was thorough and persistent in her explorations, as is evident in her aesthetigrams and commentary.

This is not to say that others without Mary's art background cannot be comparably thorough and insightful. In my 1998 article, I showed examples from two students. In the first example, the student's frustration with having to cope with a non-objective painting is evident. Her commentary implies that she had an unspoken definition of art that the painting in question does not adhere to. More familiarity with contemporary art history would have made her initial steps less difficult and perhaps prompted more adventurous interactions. But the second example, from a different student but with a similar lack of art background, showed a capacity for self-awareness and willingness to grapple with the unfamiliar that parallels Mary's interactions.

Thus I conclude that if one is sufficiently open-minded and tenacious in pursuing the meaning (to her or him), then aesthetic responses are not the exclusive purview of those with art backgrounds. Still, as Mary's work shows, previous acquaintance with art *may* give one a wider vocabulary with which to initiate meaningful interactions.

I italicized "may" in the previous sentence because previous knowledge can also be a hindrance if the person is not open to new experiences. One year I had a student who had an extensive knowledge about a particular Russian icon. When I showed the class a medieval European crucifixion painting, he rejected it because it did not conform to his notion of what a crucifixion image should look like. He imposed his view on a work that was trying to tell a different story. In short, knowledge, while generally advantageous, can be a hindrance if it results in rigidity of thinking and a lack of openness to new possibilities. Mary's "I could be wrong" statements certainly demonstrate her openness to such possibilities.

REFERENCE

Jones, R. L. Jr. (1979). Phenomenological balance and aesthetic response. *Journal of Aesthetic Education, 13*(1), 93–106.

CHAPTER FOUR

Recent Developments

Aesthetigram-Making in the Literature Classroom

AMÉLIE LEMIEUX

Acknowledgement: I would like to thank the Social Sciences and Humanities Research Council of Canada for supporting the research presented in this chapter.
—Amélie Lemieux

As we saw in earlier chapters, our epistemological stance is phenomenology based. It derives from phenomenological hermeneutics, on the premise that phenomenological accounts always precede any hermeneutical mediation (Ricoeur, 1981, 1992; Van Manen, 1990, 2014). We have previously written articles on the scope of phenomenology in addressing aesthetic experiences in visual art and museology (White, 2007, 2011, 2013, 2014) and literature (Lemieux, 2015; Lemieux & Lacelle, 2016). In this chapter, we frame this epistemology through the documentation of case studies showing three high school students' responses to literature, as documented in their aesthetigrams, ekphrastic poetry writings, and other response-induced questionnaires.

AESTHETIGRAM-MAKING IN LITERATURE CLASSES

The data we present comes from a larger mixed-methods inquiry conducted with 108 grade-11 high school students as part of their mandatory literature class. The study looked at how students produced meaning-making responses to a scene from *Incendies*, a Francophone Quebec play written by Wajdi Mouawad in 2003, and its

corresponding scene from the eponymous film adaptation, directed by Denis Villeneuve and released in 2010. In this chapter, we introduce the findings from three illus-
trative case studies meant to provide "in-depth examples" (Anderson & Arsenault,
1998, p. 155) of aesthetigram-making to shed light on traces of reader engagement.

Through this research, we observed patterns between the reader (or the *literant*,
to use Holland's 1976 term) and the art form that is experienced through the reading act. Given the multimodal essence of visual and textual art forms used in this
study (i.e., film = sound/image), we qualify the *literant* as a *multimodal literant*, a person who responds to art forms that draw upon a myriad of media. The multimodal
literant, thus, *responds* to a play (textual aspect) and a film (visual/audible aspects).
Though only one of the objects to which students responded was multimodal, their
experiences and responses to both works are multifaceted. As Csikszentmihalyi &
Robinson (1990) have pointed out, "communication with a work of art is, of course,
often a multidimensional experience, one that integrates the visual with the emotional and the intellectual" (p. 62). We support the idea that this communication is
meditated by phenomenological accounts in response to visual and written artworks,
which is why we emphasize the research strategies and tools to observe patterns of
otherwise fleeting aesthetic experiences. Thus, our study is intended to provide an
understanding of patterns of responses, which, in turn, have the potential to inform
teachers on pedagogical strategies to more fully engage students in their interactions
with literature and film. We draw from studies on meaning making through documented aesthetic experiences in response to visual art (White, 1998, 2007, 2013,
2014; White & Frois, 2013) and literature (Lemieux, 2015) to frame our research
within the parameters of aesthetigrams as a research, teaching, and learning strategy that involves a series of steps to evoke reactions and subsequent responses in
the reader-viewer. There exists a substantial difference between expressing reactions
to artworks and generating a subsequent articulated response. While the former
addresses initial and instant reactions to text, or what White (2013) calls "a private interaction between viewer and artwork" (p. 113), the latter has to do with
expressing the "reciprocal nature of the encounter" (White, 2007, p. 6). That is, the
responses describe the individual's meaning-making process, based on the reader's
originally felt reactions, sensations, feelings, impressions, and perceptions.

Aesthetic reading poses its challenges in the literature classroom. In one of her
articles, Calderwood (2005) asks a rhetorical question: "How might we respond
to a child who deeply experiences the texts of all kinds we read in the classroom"
(p. 9)? Aesthetigrams provide guidance for articulating these responses through
showing evidence of pattern recognition. Awareness of response categories help
develop rich descriptions of meaning-making (White, 2011, 2013, 2014; White &
Frois, 2013; Lemieux, 2015). And since these responses are sometimes representative of partially articulated thoughts, or what Purves and Rippere (1968) qualify as
"the tip of the iceberg," meaning that "only a small part becomes apparent to the

teacher" (Purves & Rippere, 1968, in Pantaleo, 2013, p. 125), then we must work towards elaborating tools that more fully track aesthetic experiences—examine the rest of the iceberg—to guide students in their interactions with texts.

Responses imply the ways in which one reacts to the artwork. These reactions are spontaneous and pre-reflective or, according to Abbs (1990), they consist of "intuitive apprehensions working through our senses and our feelings" (p. 252). To understand the significance and impact of student responses, teachers must resort to some sort of assessment. That is, evaluations attempt to comprehend the complex elements of responses, aesthetic, or otherwise (Abbs, 1990). In other words, both responses and evaluations are needed to get a grasp of reading engagement, since assessment of such engagement requires examination of its cognitive, affective, and aesthetic dimensions. Moreover, response to literature is a

> ... mental, emotional, intellectual, sensory, [and] physical [experience]. It encompasses the cognitive, affective, perceptual, and psychomotor activities that the reader of a poem, a story, or a novel performs as he reads or after he has read" (Purves & Rippere, 1968, p. xiii).

Researchers require tools, such as aesthetigrams, to draw attention to, and address the multifaceted nature of response. For example, aesthetigrams make evident the individual moments of responses and places them into categories determined by the reader-viewer. From the researcher/teacher's perspective, the placing into categories is a useful step beyond the tracking of individual moments of experience. The categories enable one to discern the participant's patterns of response, be they emotional, observational, symbolically disposed, and so forth. Once those patterns are evident, a teacher is then in a position to suggest strategies for broadening the experience increasingly in the direction of aesthetic response. We simply need to give ourselves to tools to access those experiences. For example, Calderwood's (2005) *Risking Aesthetic Reading* is one article that indirectly addresses the importance of looking for patterns in reader-response. In a discussion about teacher training, the article advocates elaborating "threads of descriptions, reveries, and such" (p. 7). These threads emerged as the pre-service teachers were reading and viewing the film adaptation of *Mrs. Dalloway*. Aesthetigrams fill that gap.

The facets of response Purves and Rippere describe most relate to the aesthetic dimension of reading, which has most carefully outlined by Rosenblatt (1978): "The reader who adopts the aesthetic stance can *pay attention to all of the elements activated within him by the text*, and can develop the fusion of thought and feeling ... that constitutes the integrated sensibility" (p. 46, our emphasis). That is, when one responds aesthetically, one interacts with the stimulus holistically—physically, emotionally, and intellectually (Probst, 1990). One aim of teachers is to foster increased meaning-making capacities. In the literature classroom, this requires that educators know the existing parameters of students' meaning-making capacities. Further, students' individual experiences, as expressed in their responses to literature, serve as indicators for identity construction and awareness: "Aesthetic education is about education in values awareness" (White, 2007, p. 5). Thus, students' engagement with literature is a key attribute of discovery of the self as a reader and as a student capable of meaning-making.

The goals of the study were to: (1) analyse relationships between affectively and intellectually oriented responses to generate a broader understanding of students' reading-viewing patterns; (2) provide teachers with pedagogical tools to guide students through their interactions; and (3) nurture the discourse on aesthetic experience by providing insight into its parameters and the resultant meaning-making. With the innovative combination of map-making and reading-viewing, this research provides educators with ways to bolster students' aesthetic, emotional and intellectual responses, thus creating space for equal voices through inter-subjectivity, as shown in subsequent peer discussions. Ultimately, the study calls for further investigation into alternative ways of teaching literature and film in an era where multimodality is both inevitable and ever-present.

METHODOLOGY

The larger study took place in a high school of the Greater Montreal Area, Canada. Participants had six classes of 75 minutes each, with an additional 4 hours of homework and reading at home. Over this time, participants built a portfolio in which they were asked to produce a series of exercises that would document their responses to a scene of the play *Incendies* (2003) and its corresponding scene in the 2010 eponymous film adaptation.

Incendies: Synopsis and Chosen Scene. Shortly before dying, Quebec immigrant Nawal Marwan wrote in her will she wanted her twins, 20-something Jeanne and Simon, to explore parts of the Middle East to retrace her life and that of their father and older brother. But Jeanne finds out that the real reason for her Christian mother's quest was to find out what happened to her other young son Nihad, who may have been killed in the civil war. Seeking revenge for her son's possible death, Nawal had been captured and imprisoned in the 1980s for assassinating the chief of the Christian Militia. This puzzling story leads us into the most raw and difficult parts of prison life. We discover that a prison guard repeatedly sexually assaulted her during her stay, which resulted in a pregnancy and ultimately the birth of the twins who are now investigating that past. The reader-viewer discovers as the same time as the twins that Nihad, still alive, and is both their brother and father. Simon and Jeanne find newly immigrated Canadian Nihad and give him the two letters Nawal wrote him.

We chose *Letter to the Son* (scene 37), present in both the film and play, as the prompt to which students would respond. This scene showcases emotional complexity, as it narrates a letter where a mother informs her son that she is the one he raped when he was a prison guard. We speculated that the scene would trigger vivid responses in students, given its strong emotive potential and possibilities for analysis. The original written narrative can be read as follows in the 2003 play:

Letter to the Son (Scene 37):

Simon hands his envelope to Nihad, who opens it.

NAWAL. I looked for you everywhere. Here, there, everywhere. I searched for you in the rain. I searched for you in the sun. In the forest, in the valleys, on the mountaintops, in the darkest of cities, in the darkest of streets. I searched for you in the south, in the north, in the east, in the west. I searched for you while digging in the earth to bury my friends. I searched for you while looking at the sky. I searched for you amidst a flock of birds, for you were a bird. And what is more beautiful than a bird, than a bird alone amidst the storm clouds, winging its strange destiny to the end of day? For an instant, you were horror. For an instant, you have become happiness. Horror and happiness. The silence in my throat. Do you doubt?

Let me tell you. You stood up and you took out that little clown nose. And my memory exploded. Don't be afraid. Don't catch cold. These are ancient words that come from my deepest memories. Words I often whispered to you. In my cell, I told you about your father. I told you about his face, I told you about the promise I made the day of your birth: no matter what happens, I will always love you. No matter what happens, I will always love you. Without realizing that in that very instant, you and I were sharing our defeat. Because I hated you with all my being. But where there is love, there can be no hatred. And to preserve love, I blindly chose not to speak. A she-wolf always defends her young. You are facing Janine and Simon, your sister and your brother, and since you are a child of love, they are the brother and sister of love. Listen. I am writing this letter in the cool evening air.

This letter will tell you that the woman who sings was your mother. Perhaps you too will stop talking. So be patient. I am speaking to the son, I am not speaking to the torturer. Be patient. Beyond silence, there is the happiness of being together. Nothing is more beautiful than being together. Those were your father's last words. Your mother.

Nihad finishes reading the letter. He stands.
Janine and Simon stand and face him.
Janine tears up every page in her notebook.

RESEARCH QUESTION, PORTFOLIO ELEMENTS, AND MEANING-MAKING PROCESS

We seek to answer the following research question: What traces of reader engagement can be observed through aesthetigram-making and accompanying activities as designed in this study? To answer this, we asked students to complete the following steps in the research project: (1) a pre-test evaluating reading habits; (2) a reading questionnaire assessing their comprehension of the play and film; (3) two aesthetigrams in response to a scene of the play and the film (directions were provided to guide students on the mapping process and procedures); (4) a written *ekphrastic* response (poem, short story, or letter) corresponding to each of their two maps; and (6) a post-test that explored their map-making impressions and accompanying awareness of their aesthetic responses. While students could take as much time as they wanted to read the play at home prior to the project, the film was projected during class hours. For those students who were absent during the original in-class screening, we lent them a copy of the film that they could watch at home.

AESTHETIGRAM-MAKING

Students were introduced to the aesthetigram concept during the first day of the project. They had to follow multiple steps in order to complete an aesthetigram. In the preliminary phase, we designed the steps and visually reproduced them in a PowerPoint presentation that we showed students. The following steps were introduced and accomplished:

1. Writing down consecutive numbered reactions to the chosen scene written play.
2. Attributing to each reaction a degree of importance, i.e. How impactful was the reaction for the reader?
3. Reading through the list of categories that we provided for them. The categories include, for example, "Imagination," "Emotion," "Preference," "Judgement," "Reflection," "Reverie," "Comparison," and so on.
4. Classifying each reaction in a category of the list (e.g., Judgement I, Reflection II, Memory II). The Roman numbers indicate a sub-category of the main category. If the reaction could not be classified in one of the pre-determined categories, then the reader could create her/his own by explaining how it differed from those that were available.
5. Color-coding the reactions according to their respective categories in order to visually situate them in their aesthetigram.
6. Transcribing each category-coded reaction on coloured sticky notes corresponding to the code established in step 5.
7. Sticking the notes to a blank sheet of paper.
8. Moving the notes around to establish links between the different reactions (e.g., this reaction led to this one, or these reactions are grouped as they are from the same category).

Students repeated these steps to draw their aesthetigram in response to the corresponding scene of the film. The two completed aesthetigrams were included in their portfolio. We provide examples of completed aesthetigrams and accompanying ekphrastic writing in the data section of this chapter.

EKPHRASTIC WRITING

Building upon historical etymology, Krieger (1998) defines ekphrasis as "the verbal equivalent of a plastic art object" (p. 4). Likewise, Heffernan (1998) says ekphrasis is "verbal articulation of a visual representation" (p. 191). These definitions may appear to suggest that ekphrasis is a form of imitation. But ekphrasis is not an imitation of the original visual stimulus. An imitation would be doomed to failure. For example, if one were to attempt to simply describe a sunset, the result could not help but be a weak cousin to the original. Instead, ekphrasis is an artistic writing endeavour—often poetry—that uses a visual work as its springboard for its own original creation. That creation is an elaboration upon the individual's viewing experience and

> may take a number of directions, only one of which is a specific reference to discrete features of an artwork. Others could be: an emulation of the work's structure to evoke a similar mood; a commentary or philosophic stance that reflects the viewer's response to the work in terms of its personal and social significance; or combinations of these foci. (White, 2013, p. 110)

A well-known example is Pieter Breughel's *Landscape with the Fall of Icarus* (1558) as interpreted quite differently, one from the other, by twentieth century poets William Carlos Williams and W. H. Auden. Where Williams is quite faithful to the painting's details, Auden veers from it to make a philosophical statement about humanity's indifference to suffering.

In my (Amélie's) project, the participants' challenge was to not only track the moments of their responses to the play and the film but subsequently to attempt their own creative work.

We submit that ekphrasis has the potential to generate deeper aesthetic engagement in readers and viewers. For ekphrasis calls upon the ability to distinguish between one's self and the artwork, creating a necessary distance to better infuse, or recreate, that attachment to the text[1] through poetry. The relationship with reading and viewing makes sense. When students read a book, some of them will get immersed in the narrative, and upon reflection, they will most likely see elements that differ from their experiences or that resembles them: "it is primarily through my engagement with what is not me that I effect the integration of my senses, and thereby experience my own unity and coherence" (Abram, 1996, p. 125). That is, ekphrastic writing allows oneself to be immersed in one's phenomenological thoughts by using writing to reproduce the expressions of various modalities—in our case, text, and film.

Over the last decade, ekphrastic writing has been the subject of many art education studies, notably because this type of articulation bolsters student voice (White, 2013) and calls upon students' senses (Howell, 2011; Mansoor, 2014; Moorman, 2006). For example, in a recent study on the ways of incorporating ekphrasis in *English as a Second Language* classrooms, Mansoor (2014) found that students were not only engaging their senses in the activities, but it provided them with new ways of exploring personal writings that were anchored in their experiences of artworks. In light of this research, it appears that, for students, ekphrastic writing is another avenue to aesthetic experiences, a reinvestment in writing that derives from a vivid evocation of the artwork. In other words, ekphrastic poetry allows readers to compare their own responses to that of artworks through a synergetic articulation of their perception of that artwork (Kjeldsen, 2001). The benefits of ekphrastic writing have been corroborated by Sager Eidt (2008): "Analyzing the literary and filmic reception and concretization of a work of art through their ekphrases, we can gain insight into the similarities and differences in the interpretation of famous works of art in high and in popular culture." (p. 19) Ultimately, ekphrastic writing benefits readers and viewers, in that it provides them with creative tools to express their perceptions of the artworks. As one participant explained in the study, it allows the reader to generate "other knowledge about" what is experienced.

If one of the postulates of reader response is to encourage discourse—and transactions—with the text, then one strategy that guides students in doing so is certainly ekphrastic poetry, for "ekphrasis offers art educators a rich potential for individual efforts at meaning-making and shared experience" (White, 2013, p. 113). Moreover, for some students, reading can be a vicarious synesthetic experience (Abram, 1996) and deepen the capacity to experience the world through one's imagination (Lemieux & Lacelle, 2016; Nussbaum, 1998; Swanger, 2013; Wiebe, 2013). It is within these spaces, and in lieu of physical experience, that "mental images" occur (Brehm, 2008; Langlade, 2006). Further, these images allow students to conceptualize their vision of the work and make connections with past experiences—what they know best: "in making connections, students begin to recognize—to know again—that their own active imaginations enrich their learning, give breadth to their writing and thinking, and let them experience that they are the creators of context" (Rico in Moorman, 2006, p. 52). And so, to us, whether the aesthetic object is a visual or written artwork matters not; an articulation of the perceptive milieu through ekphrastic writing will certainly provide ways to meaning-making.

With this rationale, in the study with high school students, we asked them to follow clear guidelines to produce ekphrastic writing, after they had drawn their aesthetigrams. Some students found that aesthetigram-making was helpful in order to do the writing activity.

The guidelines for producing ekphrastic poetry were as follows:

> In this document, write a poem, prose or a short story that echoes your experience with regards to each of your aesthetigrams. You will then have to justify the chosen format (poem prose, short story) and explain the style and content you chose. For example, a poem provides a more flexible mode of expression and this could be part of your answer. The goal is to formulate your aesthetic experience of the scene through a written form and to reproduce your felt reactions when reading and viewing the scene. You may reuse words from your aesthetigram in your writing. The aesthetigram is meant to situate your reactions, and the writing is meant to comment on and express this experience.

I then provided students with an example, reproduced from White's (2013) study on his aesthetic experiences and ekphrastic writings in response to the painting *Yellow Street II* by Lionel Feininger (1918), as a starting point, an inspiration to start writing their own.

Below we show the example of a male student who provides insight into the use of aesthetigrams as a phenomenological research tool to show traces of reader engagement.

DATA: PETER'S READING ENGAGEMENT AND HABITS

Peter described himself as a reader who is inclined to read works from authors he likes, that he reads easily, without help, and likes discussing with friends and family. He is moderately reflective on the content (3 points out of 6, where 6 = very similar to my habits, and 1 = very far from my habits), and he almost never uses reading strategies when reading (e.g., highlighting text, making summaries, writing notes in the margins). This student liked reading the play, he gave a rating of 5 on 6 (where 6 = I adored reading the play), and explained that he really enjoys watching film adaptations in class (6/6). He also enjoys writing creative pieces in school contexts (6/6). Peter is therefore a good example of a student generally interested in reading. He does not represent the typical struggling male reader that is often portrayed in reading research.

For Peter, being engaged in reading means: "reading a book and picturing the story in my mind. When engaged, I know the character's emotions and can imagine their storyline as if I was there. I can feel something if something bad happens to the protagonists. An engaged reader will only notice all the pages he has read when he is already at the last page."

Reactions to the Written Play:

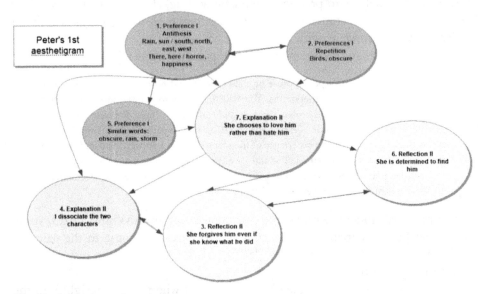

Fig 4.1. Aesthetigram 1.
Source: Author's dissertation data.

ACCOMPANYING COMMENTARY FOR THE FIRST AESTHETIGRAM

I put reaction 7 in the middle of my aesthetigram because it is the most important one for me. I think it is the central theme of the scene. I placed the three preferences reactions together because they are less important than the four others. They are linked together because they share the same goal, which is to enrich the text. I linked the antithesis to the fourth reaction because with the two reactions, I think there is a strong link. I think Nawal makes comparisons between the rain and the father, and between the sun and the son. By distinguishing the two characters (# 4), Nawal can forgive the son for what he has done. She forgives the son because, for her, it's not the same people (who committed the crime).

REMARKS

Despite having explained in great detail the purpose and use of the links between the categories, which are to establish relationships and causalities between reactions, there seems to have been a misunderstanding in Peter's aesthetigram. That is, perhaps the link between reactions 6 and 7 should have been from 6 to 7 rather than the reverse, for the sixth logically precedes the seventh. The same pattern can be observed for reactions 7 and 3.

Furthermore, Peter placed his "preferences" and "reflections" respectively at the top and bottom of his aesthetigram. Peter maintained that the most central idea was his last one, an "explanation" reaction, in which the mother chooses to love her son rather than hate him. We note that he created three links that go to #7 (#1, 2, and 5), and three that depart from the seventh category to reach #3, #4, and #6.

EKPHRASIS IN RESPONSE TO THE FIRST AESTHETIGRAM (LITERATURE)

The choice is hard to make. What image of you should I keep? The torturer who made me suffer the most atrocious affliction or the son that I have been looking for and that I finally found? I think there is good in each person, so for me, you are not the torturer. You are the son that I have been looking for during all these years in the country where it all began. If I am speaking to the son, happiness replaces horror. Our children represent love and joy.

Peter's Comment: The letter to the son in the book has to do with the fact that she asks herself how to perceive Nihad as her son. I chose this form because it allows me to show what I have felt as if I was in Nawal's shoes.

REMARKS

Peter asked two pivotal questions in his first ekphrastic prose that do not explicitly reflect that of its central reaction in his first aesthetigram (#7, mother's love predominates hate). However, in the subsequent phrases, he addressed that in seventh reaction by asserting "there is good in each person ... If I am speaking to the son, happiness replaces horror." While in his aesthetigram, Peter expresses his preference for cardinal points (#1), repetitions (#2), and climate metaphors (#5), he did not extrapolate these themes in his poem. He rather focussed on Nawal's felt reactions, as he explained in his personal comment.

Reactions to the Film

ACCOMPANYING COMMENTARY FOR THE SECOND AESTHETIGRAM

I put reaction 4 in the middle because it was the most important for me. I put reaction 1 far from the other ones because it has a weaker link with other categories. I linked reaction 2 and 7 because I think that reaction 7 caused Nihad's reaction. Reactions 2 and 5 are related because they are very similar. Reactions 3 and 6 are linked because both of them have to do with Jeanne and Simon. Nawal reassures Nihad by telling him she loves her kids even though they are born from pain. I chose to put reactions 3-4-6-7 in the reflections category because I reflected on Nihad and Nawal's actions.

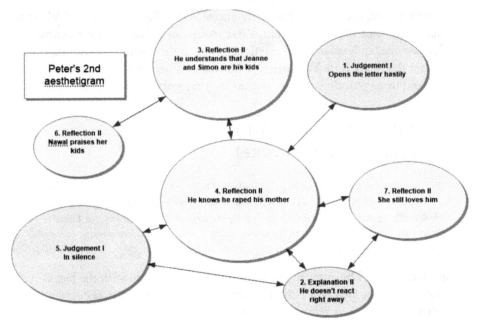

Fig 4.2. Aesthetigram 2.
Source: Author's dissertation data).

REMARKS

In his second aesthetigram, Peter expressed more reactions he categorized as reflections. Again, subsequent reactions, including his central one (#4), are linked to previous ones (e.g., #3, #2). While these links are not chronological, Peter did construct meaning out of them, as he noted in his commentary "#2 and #5 are related because they are very similar." Beyond identifying similarities in reactions, Peter established links between his reflections and his judgements, and even causalities (#2 and #7). This process generates meaning-making awareness of his responses to the scene of the film.

EKPHRASIS IN RESPONSE TO THE SECOND AESTHETIGRAM (FILM)

How can you continue to love me after all I did to you? Without knowing, you already found me. You looked for me all your life and when you saw me again for the first time, we did not recognize each other. Maybe it was better that way. I saw our kids that you find so endearing. How could you say that? They are born from an atrocious rape and from pain! For me, it is impossible to see the good side of things and happiness for everyone. It is really hard to live knowing what I did to you.

Peter's Comment: I wrote a text from Nihad's point of view because in the two stories we don't really know what he is thinking about. From his point of view, Nihad reacts to the letter he receives from his mother and comments on it.

REMARKS

Written from Nihad's point of view, Peter's second ekphrasis corresponds to what I call the "after," that is, Nihad's potentially imagined reactions. For example "How could you say that?" is a question that comes after the reflections Peter makes in his aesthetigram about Nihad's actions. Peter wrote his prose in the first person, and provided the reader with expressions materialized through punctuation (i.e., question and exclamation marks). It is interesting to note that the overall feeling the reader is left with is that of despair—"it is really hard to live"—a feeling or an impression that cannot be accessed by the viewer when watching the film. Peter took this writing opportunity to extrapolate on his perception of the scene.

POST-TEST RESULTS

Film adaptations can help readers be more engaged in reading a book as they provide opportunities to compare elements between both narratives. The most prevalent categories of Peter's first aesthetigram were: Preferences I, Explanation II, and Reflection II. The "preferences" category was predominant because he appreciated the elements that were most evident in his reading. It was a question of taste. In fact, Peter could have included a "taste" category as a *co-intended* (consciously experienced) moment. But he may not have made the connection between taste and preferences.

For the second aesthetigram, the categories were: Reflection II, Judgement I, and Explanation II. He explained that Reflections were more numerous because he asked himself questions about Nawal's and Nihad's thoughts.

OVERALL OCCURRENCES FOR EACH CATEGORIES IN BOTH AESTHETIGRAMS

Preferences I	Explanation II	Reflection II	Judgement I
3	3	6	2

He explained that aesthetigrams helped him reflect on and analyse further his reading by asking himself why Nawal still loved Nihad after what he did. Peer discussions allowed him to realize that his peers "had pretty much the same reactions" as he did, except that "some of them had emotional reactions," which he did not experience. "By making an aesthetigram, we can reflect more on, and pay attention to, our reactions. We can also make links between categories and elements [of the play and the film]." Thus, Peter's assessment of the contributions of aesthetigram-making was positive. He asserted that he would make aesthetigrams again in French classes, for both novels, plays, and film adaptations. Peter was also able to see the advantages of doing more than one aesthetigram. The comparison between #1 and #2 enabled him to see his evolving engagement.

DATA: TIM'S READING ENGAGEMENT AND HABITS

Tim qualifies himself as a person who generally does not enjoy reading, that he does not read easily or voluntarily, and that he has had trouble being focused while reading. He never uses reading strategies when reading (1 out of 6 points), but rates his reflection abilities on the content as being very high (6 out of 6 points). Tim moderately enjoyed reading *Incendies* (3 points out of 6), but really likes watching film adaptations (6/6). He finds creative writing to be extremely boring (1/6).

Finally, Tim does not enjoy sharing his thoughts on his reading with friends and family. Tim describes reading engagement as "reading on a regular basis." Compared to Peter's definition (picturing the story in my mind), one could argue that his definition of reading engagement is limited.

Reactions to the Written Play

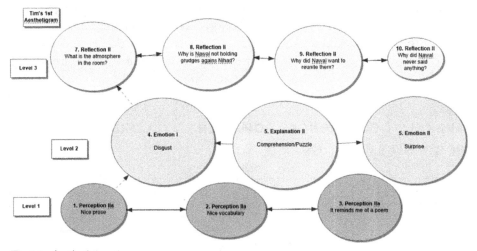

Fig 4.3. Aesthetigram 1.
Source: Author's dissertation data.

ACCOMPANYING COMMENTARY FOR THE FIRST AESTHETIGRAM

My aesthetigram can be read from the bottom to the top. You can read my reactions in a chronological manner. I first noticed the writing style. I noticed the author used nice prose and vocabulary. The text reminded me of a poem. I put these three reactions together, linked to the rest with a dashed arrow because I did not feel they fit with the rest of my reactions. When I continued reading, I started to understand what happened with Nawal and Nihad. That is when I felt disgust and surprise. That is why I put arrows that go from comprehension to the emotions I felt by understanding the situation. These three elements are central, because they made me react the most. After reading the scene, I asked myself a lot of questions. I asked myself what was the atmosphere in the room when the secret was unveiled. How could Nawal not be upset with Nihad? Why did Nawal want to bring together her three kids? And why didn't she say anything before? I thus put these three reactions together and they are on top of my aesthetigram as they are really important.

REMARKS

Tim provided extensive details in the commentary accompanying his first aesthetigram. He demonstrates a high level of logic in his discourse. For example, his aesthetigram is divided into three levels, indicating structure in ideas and responses: "My aesthetigram can be read from the bottom to the top. You can read my reactions in a chronological manner." Very logically, Tim's aesthetigram goes from perceptions (pre-reflective) to emotions/explanations (reflection in process), and it finishes with reflections (final understandings). His accompanying commentary reflects the reasoning of his discourse and his map-making.

EKPHRASIS IN RESPONSE TO THE FIRST AESTHETIGRAM (LITERATURE)

Long ago, she was imprisoned,
However, she forgave
Behind bars, she was impregnated
Her beloved child
Was with her without pity
However, she forgot
He raped her without hesitation
He broke her
She, on the other hand,
Did not collapse
She continued to love
A motherly love for her baby

Is not fleeting, but solid as a rock
Because even hate can't stop it
But how can we forgive
Such atrocities

Tim's Comment: My poem is on my reflection, which aimed at asking myself how Nawal could not feel resentment towards Nihad. I decided to write a poem on that question, because this genre inspired me and provided me with more creativity.

REMARKS

In his short ekphrastic poem, Tim adopted a very brief, yet rich style of writing. He used repetitions (e.g., "However, she") that mark strong oppositions that can be felt in the emotions section of his first aesthetigram. The poem leaves the impression that it depicts a conversation—a tug-of-war—between mother/son, Nawal/Nihad, prisoner/rapist. The question of forgiveness is left to the very end of the poem, where "she" is transformed into "we." This change calls for inclusion of the collective comprised of the author of the poem and its reader, and asks perhaps rhetorically the actions that can be forgiven ("how can we forgive such atrocities?"). Indeed, in his accompanying comment, Tim referred to his questioning: "My poem is on my reflection, which aimed at asking myself how Nawal could not feel resentment towards Nihad."

Reactions to the Film

ACCOMPANYING COMMENTARY FOR THE
SECOND AESTHETIGRAM

My first reaction was incomprehension, because I immediately asked myself why Nawal wanted to bring her three kids together. Then, when she read the letter in the film, I felt sadness, pity, dismay, and disgust. Together, these four reactions are the strongest. That is why I grouped them in the centre to emphasize their importance. Then, when Nawal enumerates all the places she has been to look for her son, I felt her determination and despair. Finally, I noticed that the oral narration was well done, and it also reminded me of a poem. These three reactions are aside in the bottom, because they are just observations. They were reactions that were less personal and less important for me.

REMARKS

Tim's second aesthetigram provided insights into the most important reactions he felt when he viewed the same scene from the film adaptation. To create an

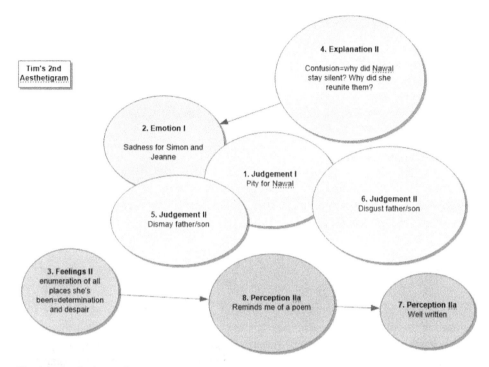

Fig 4.4. Aesthetigram 2.
Source: Author's dissertation data.

effect of cohesion, he juxtaposed them into a central theme. Contrary to his first aesthetigram, perceptions and feelings are seen as "observations", which he places at the bottom right corner of his map. He saw them as being "aside," and purposefully places them that way as he considers they do not fit well with the rest of his map. Despite this organization, the link between reaction #4 and #2 is not clearly explained, and creates gaps in comprehension. However, in the commentary Tim explained that his first reaction was incomprehension, which is represented by his fourth reaction in the aesthetigram. Perhaps his numbers were mismatched in this case.

EKPHRASIS IN RESPONSE TO THE SECOND AESTHETIGRAM (FILM)

Disgust and dismay were my first reactions
When my mind linked them together
Father and son are the same token
In this inconceivable union
When you will open this letter

You were struck by stupefaction
I then felt satisfaction
Because that's all he deserves that stupid man
You cultivated hate
You collected shame
This does not sadden me.
That's how life goes.
You are now dishonored
You well deserved it
There is nowhere to hide and rest

Comment: I have decided, once again, to write a poem because by reflecting on my rhymes that the ideas came to mind. My poem is on the disgust I felt towards Nihad as I understood he raped his mother.

REMARKS

Tim's second ekphrastic poem is as brief as his first one. It is profoundly felt, nonetheless. Interestingly, Tim started the poem with his own reactions, and the first three lines of the poem directly express relations between the writing and the aesthetigram. It is a very subjective and personal piece, the reader does not feel detached from the lived experiences of the writer. Rather, compared to the first ekphrases we saw, the writing provides phenomenological insights into the meaning-making and felt reactions of the initial reader, who is the author in this case.

POST-TEST RESULTS

I noted that film adaptations can help readers be more engaged in reading a book, as film involves more of the physical senses. Therefore, although Tim feels that films "require less concentration," it is more a matter of reading requiring more imagination in order to attain a similar level of sensory involvement.

I observed that the most prevalent categories of his first aesthetigram were: Emotions I, Explanation II, Perception II, and Reflection II. Tim emphasized his emotional reactions by placing those moments in the middle of the aesthetigram.

For the second aesthetigram, the categories were: Emotions I, Judgement II, Feelings II, Perception II, and Explanation II. He explained that Judgement elements prevailed. Emotions were less present since he already knew what would happen. Our thoughts on this are that, arguably, Tim's judgements were primarily affectively laden. That is, "dismay," "pity," and "disgust" are not exclusively rational, disinterested responses. By this, we mean that we was likely more involved than he realized.

OVERALL OCCURRENCES FOR EACH CATEGORY IN BOTH AESTHETIGRAMS

Explanation II	Reflection II	Perception II	Emotions I	Judgement II	Feelings II
2	4	5	2	3	1

Aesthetigrams helped him understand, appreciate, reflect on, interpret, and analyse the written scene. A reason for this, he explains, is that he had not considered, or paid attention to, the ways he reacted before doing this activity. Peer discussions allowed him to realize that he felt more emotional reactions than his peers. The second aesthetigram seemed redundant for this participant, for he felt his reactions were the same. It was "difficult to find new reactions after knowing what happened."

DATA: WILL'S READING ENGAGEMENT AND HABITS

As a reader, Will explains he is inclined to read works from authors he likes, that he reads easily, without help, and that he is focussed when reading. He reads voluntarily at times (3 points out of 6), and he never uses reading strategies when reading. He admits he reflects sufficiently on the content he reads. This student liked reading the play, he gave a rating of 5 on 6 (where 6 = I adored reading the play), and explained that he moderately enjoys watching film adaptations in class (4/6). He also really enjoys writing creative pieces in school contexts (6/6).

For Will, reading engagement means: "being able to read without feeling school pressure or mandatory assignments. It is also being motivated to read without liking it. Because there are lots of positive points like making less mistakes in writing, developing creative skills, and spending time alone reflecting and relaxing." Will's statement that reading engagement is feeling "motivated to read without liking it," but with foreseen advantages like improvement in writing skills makes us think that reading is seen as standardized process, or what Sarroub & Pernicek (2016) call "a focus on teaching isolated reading skills, such as decoding, fluency, and basic comprehension" (p. 50). The authors note that this process works against reading engagement. We think that Will is an example of a student's voice that represents this finding.

Reactions to the Written Play

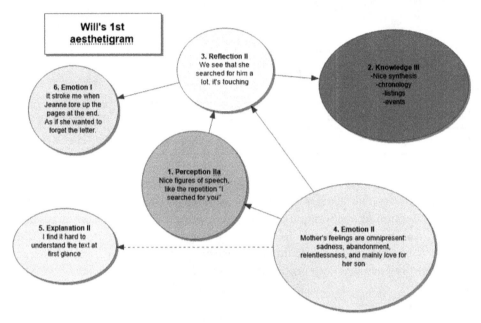

Fig 4.5. Aesthetigram 1.
Source: Author's dissertation data.

ACCOMPANYING COMMENTARY FOR THE FIRST AESTHETIGRAM

I put in the centre the emotions that I felt because that is what emerged from my reactions to the *Letter to the Son*. My reactions are really striking and they really impacted me. The figures of speech like the repetition of "I looked for you" were numerous in the letter, I think they make the reading more enjoyable. Also, it allowed us to see that she looked for him quite a bit. That was an important moment in the *Letter to the Son* in my eyes. I really liked the fact that the letter was well structured. She enumerates the most important events (synthesis) and it allowed me to follow the events. I found another part of the letter that was somewhat relevant: when Jeanne tears up the pages at the end. A little reaction that I put with a dashed arrow was that I had trouble understanding some parts of the letter at the first glance.

REMARKS

Will's first aesthetigram is quite detailed and varied reaction-wise. Each reaction falls within a different category, with the exception of the "emotions" category. His commentary remarks go from being focussed on the emotions, to targeting style and form. His meaning-making articulates that the structure of the letter helped him understand the narrative, and that his emotions granted him access to structure awareness.

EKPHRASIS IN RESPONSE TO THE FIRST AESTHETIGRAM (LITERATURE)

The feeling of sadness overpowered my soul
Like a blade
Cutting through my flesh
I was not expecting seeing you again.
I then mourned your death
However, abandoning you was no solution
I had to continue
I searched for you all my life
I never ran out of love to give,
How did I do that?
I promised myself that I would not give up
I lived through solitude
And I would not live this adventure again, for nothing in the world.

Comment: I chose to write a poem with prose as I did not want to constrain myself with only matching rhymes. I must say, though, that I put some matching rhymes here and there to make my writing nicer. My priority, in this text, was to demonstrate how the mother had a difficult time finding her son. How did she manage not to lose hope?

REMARKS

Like Tim, Will's ekphrastic writing takes the form of a short poem. It emphasizes the moment when Nawal looks for Nihad and embodies hope in that search. The repetitive use of "I" perhaps echoes the notion of style Will originally depicted in his aesthetigram. Recurring themes between the aesthetigram and the poem include: the mother's search for her son, sadness, abandonment, not giving up (relentlessness), and her love for her son.

Reactions to the Film

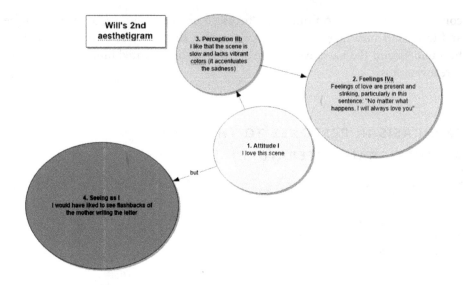

Fig 4.6. Aesthetigram 2.
Source: Author's dissertation data.

ACCOMPANYING COMMENTARY FOR THE SECOND AESTHETIGRAM

I placed in the centre the fact that I like this scene because it was really striking to see how it was filmed. It was recorded in a very slow pace, with dark colours so we could see that it was a very serious and sad scene, just like the characters who played it. What's more touching than the mother's unconditional love for her son, she will love him forever, no matter what happens. I found this part to be touching. Finally, I would have liked, however, to be presented with flashbacks to show us how it went about when she wrote the letter. She must have found it difficult to look for her son and not find him.

REMARKS

Will's second aesthetigram is less detailed than his first one. In fact, it is one of the less detailed ones gathered in the data for this study. Will's last reaction is his most important one, while the one he placed in the centre does not benefit from much attention. For Will, emphasis is placed on what he would have liked to see in the film rather than the fact that he identify he loved the scene. This gives insight into his narrative imagination (Langlade, 2006; Nussbaum, 1998), that is, he would have appreciated seeing flashbacks as Nawal narrated the scene. This example shows that aesthetigrams can give lieu to further engagement by looking at how students go beyond their initial preferences to generate content and ideas themselves. If we consider that narrative imagination is a trace of reading engagement, then aesthetigrams help move students in that direction.

EKPHRASIS IN RESPONSE TO THE SECOND AESTHETIGRAM (FILM)

At the edge of despair,
I would have loved to see you again
To hold you in my arms
To caress you here and there
It is all I ever wanted
A last thought that had now died
Like my soul, severely wounded by life
This filthy life that gets darker with time
You were my last hope
My last hope to live again
I had trouble believing it
I was destined to lie hidden in this vault
However, don't forget that
This sentence that crosses my mind night and day
This sentence that is not morose:
No matter what happens, I will always love you.

Will's Comment: I chose to write a poem because I wanted to try something new and also because I think it is more appropriate to use this genre to write something sad. I wanted to emphasize the fact that the mother liked her son a lot despite the fact that she had trouble finding him.

REMARKS

In his second poem, Will recreated his aesthetigram with the intention of showing how Nawal loved her son. The themes he chose to write about are thus similar to Tim's. However, he adopted a different style of writing and, instead of taking elements from his aesthetigram, he rewrote a phrase from the text, which he identified as a reaction in his aesthetigram "no matter what happens, I will always love you," arguably the most repeated and important sentence of the scene. Unlike the elements he drew in his aesthetigram, Will did not pursue the idea of exploring "flashbacks" in his poem, nor did he address the colours of pace he originally felt, as documented in his aesthetigram.

POST-TEST RESULTS

As was the case with Tim, I noted that the film adaptation helped Will as well. I observed that the most prevalent categories of his first aesthetigram were: Emotions I & II, Reflection II, Knowledge III, Perception IIa, and Explanation II. He justified his mapping process by noting that the emotions category was the most predominant because there were a lot of emotions implied in the text.

For the second aesthetigram, the categories were: Perception IIb, Attitude I, Feelings IV, and Imagination I. He explained that there were no predominant categories in this particular case.

OVERALL OCCURRENCES FOR EACH CATEGORIES IN BOTH AESTHETIGRAMS

Emotions I and II	Perception IIa and b	Explanation II, Knowledge III, Attitude I, Reflection II, Feelings IV, Imagination I
2	2	1

He explained that aesthetigrams clarified for him the scene "The Letter to the Son," but that the exercise was limited to that clarification. He found the second aesthetigram to be redundant, as it "was the same thing." He did not necessarily enjoy the aesthetigram activity, but he really appreciated producing ekphrastic writing as "it provided a creative outlet to write an alternative ending to the scene." In his second aesthetigram, Will confirmed his initial gestalt response. The fact that he notes fewer moments in the second aesthetigram indicates a rapid move towards his gestalt response, not traces of disengagement. Moment #3 shows an awareness of the importance of form in the construction of the story. Reaction #1 was a potentially missed opportunity for him to explore what it was he "loved" about the scene, that is, his tastes and values.

LIMITATIONS

In this particular study, the limitations are that the project was conducted over several weeks rather than several months. This implies that students' sustained reading engagement was not covered due to time constraints on the part of the school. However, we offer a snapshot of what aesthetigrams can provide for reading engagement.

On a more global view, we address the topic of the usefulness of aesthetic experiences for reading engagement. While it is not specifically he object of this chapter, debates around the nature of the aesthetic experience will always be perpetuated in discussions about art criticism and reception, especially in educational contexts. White (1998) covered some of these topics, for example, dichotomies in conversations between aestheticians and art educators, in the introduction of his first article on aesthetigrams. Some of the ongoing conversations revolve around the idea that aesthetic experiences cannot be measured, for they are fleeting and evanescent. With this chapter, we have proven otherwise. We know that aesthetic experiences are time-bound and fixed in time (Dewey, 1934/2005). They are moments of particular individual significance.

With aesthetigrams, we are giving ourselves tools to measure what some art critics say is unmeasurable, a valuable effort in itself in research about reception. Aesthetigrams are not a deterrent to aesthetic experiences. In other words, when the participant becomes aware of the individual moments of experience, the aesthetic nature of the experience is heightened, not interfered with. The time spent in front of an artwork during a museum visit is, on average, a few seconds. For example, a recent survey conducted at the Tate Britain Museum showed that visitors spent less than five seconds contemplating Tracey Emin's and Damien Hirst's works (Hensher, 2013). To counter these types of statistics, the aesthetigram exercise obliges participants to slow down, take note of their reactions, and become increasingly more self-aware. In the case studies, we showed that this could also be made possible with text and film, and the reflections on aesthetigram-making through commentary and ekphrastic writing could lead to traces of engagement.

CONCLUSION

This chapter provides documentation of detailed experiences of three male students through their aesthetigrams, ekphrastic writings, and accompanying commentary. We offered further remarks regarding students' work as to their respective engagement. We maintain that aesthetigrams point to students' values in regard to their likes and dislikes. Ultimately, our findings corroborate what we have found in previous studies (White, 2007, 2011, 2013, 2014; Lemieux, 2015; Lemieux & Lacelle, 2016).

This study is deeply rooted in Rosenblatt's work (1994), who spent a lifetime's work theorizing her transactional theory of reading, which distinguishes the aesthetic from the efferent stances in the processes of reading. The efferent stance takes place when the "attention is centred predominantly on what is to be extracted and retained after the reading event" (p. 11). In other words, it is meant to identify what the terms signify in order to take action in the future. It is based on facts of the narrative, or what we commonly refer to as the 5 *W*'s (who, when, what, why, where—and how). The aesthetic stance, on the other hand, refers to "the qualities of the feelings, ideas, situations, scenes, personalities, and emotions that are called forth" (Rosenblatt, 1994, p. 11) in the reading process. Both stances operate, according to Rosenblatt, on a continuum. We showed traced of that continuum in students' reading experiences, which they documented in their respective aesthetigrams.

Finally, this study showed the applicability of aesthetigrams to research, teaching, and learning. Stemming from a "pedagogical intuition" (White, 1998, p. 321) and intended to "improve teaching and learning in regard to aesthetics-in-the-classroom" (*ibid*), aesthetigrams were first conceived for instructive purposes to know more about students' experiences with visual art. The process was meant to provide ways to increase awareness of moments of experience. In other studies (White, 2013), it was used uniquely as a self-teaching device. We argue that insofar as participants become aware of their patterns of response, they can deliberately focus on enlarging the range of their experiences. Lemieux (2015) demonstrated classroom-based applications of this in a study with female high school students responding to literature. As research strategies, aesthetigrams have been used in several studies (White, 2007, 2011, 2014; White and Frois, 2013) that showed the usefulness of values awareness in responding to art. We develop these aspects further in subsequent chapters of this book.

NOTE

1. By text, we do not imply a one-dimensional definition that only includes written text. Rather, we mainly adopt the well-documented multifaceted definition used in countless studies (Bodgan et al., 1997; Lebrun et al., 2012; Rowsell, 2014). In line with these studies, we thus define "text" by means of an all-encompassing definition including traditional print narratives as well as multimodal ones, like film adaptations.

REFERENCES

Abbs, P. (1991). Defining the aesthetic field. In R. A. Smith and A. Simpson (Eds.). *Aesthetics and Arts Education* (pp. 245–255). Urbana and Chicago, IL: University of Illinois Press.

Abram, D. (1996). *The spell of the sensuous: Perception and language in a more-than-human world*. New York, NY: Vintage Books.

Anderson, G. & Arsenault, N. (1998). *Fundamentals of educational research* (2nd edition). Philadelphia, PA: The Falmer Press Teachers' Library, Taylor & Francis.

Bodgan, D., Davis, H. E., & Robertson, J. (1997). Sweet surrender and trespassing desires in reading: Jane Campion's *The Piano* and the struggle for responsible pedagogy. *Changing English, 4*(1), 81–103.

Brehm, S. (2008). Le rôle de l'imaginaire dans le processus de référenciation. *Figura, 20,* 31–44.

Calderwood, P. (2005). Risking aesthetic reading. *International Journal of Education & the Arts, 6*(3), 1–11.

Csikszentmihalyi, M. & Robinson, R. E. (1990). *The art of seeing: An interpretation of the aesthetic encounter.* Malibu, CA: Getty Trust Office of Publications.

Dery, L. & McCraw K. (producers) & Villeneuve, D. (Director). (2010). *Incendies* [Motion Picture]. Canada & France: Sony Pictures Classics.

Dewey, J. (1934/2005). *Art as experience.* New York: Penguin.

Feininger, L. (1918). *Yellow Street* [Oil on canvas]. Montreal Museum of Fine Arts, Permanent Collection, Montreal, QC.

Heffernan, J. A. W. (1998). Entering the museum of words: Ashbery's 'Self-Portrait in a convex mirror.' In Robillard, V. & E. Jongeneel (Eds.), *Pictures into words: Theoretical and descriptive approaches to ekphrasis* (pp. 189–211). Amsterdam, The Netherlands: VU University Press.

Hensher, P. (2011, March 13). We know what we like, and it's not modern art! How gallery visitors only viewed work by Damien Hirst and Tracey Emin for less than 5 seconds. *The Daily Mail.* Retrieved at: http://www.dailymail.co.uk/news/article-1365672/Modern-art-How-gallery-visitors-viewed-work-Damien-Hirst-Tracy-Emin-5-seconds.html

Holland, N. (1976). New paradigm: Subjective or transactive? *New Literary History, 7*(2), 335–346.

Howell, J. S. (2011). *Implications of classroom writing instruction emphasizing imagination, creativity, and dialogue: A case study.* Unpublished doctoral thesis, Kent State University.

Kjeldsen, J. (2001). What can the aesthetic movement tell us about aesthetic education? *Journal of Aesthetic Education, 31*(1), 85–97.

Krieger, M. (1998). The problem of ekphrasis: Images and words, space and time—and the literary work. In V. Robillard, & E. Jongeneel (Eds.), *Pictures into words: Theoretical and descriptive approaches to ekphrasis* (pp. 3–20). Amsterdam, Netherlands: VU University Press.

Langlade, G. (2006). L'activité fictionnalisante du lecteur. In M. Braud, B. Laville, & B. Louichon (Eds.). *Les enseignements de la fiction.* Bordeaux: Presses de l'Université de Bordeaux.

Lebrun, M., Lacelle, N., & Boutin, J.-F. (2012). Genèse et essor du concept de littératie médiatique multimodale. *Mémoires du livre/Studies in Book Culture, 3*(2), 1–24, http://www.erudit.org/revue/memoires/2012/v3/n2/1009351ar.html#no2

Lemieux, A. (2015). Think it *through*: Fostering aesthetic experiences to raise interest in literature at the high school level. *Journal of the Canadian Association for Curriculum Studies, 12*(2), 66–93.

Lemieux, A. & Lacelle, N. (2016). Approches transactionnelle, subjective, et phénoménologique en didactique de la lecture. *Myriades, 2*(1), 14–28. http://cehum.ilch.uminho.pt/myriades/static/volumes/2–2.pdf

Mansoor, A. (2014). Ekphrastic practices in catalysing creative writing in undergraduate ESL classrooms. *International Journal for the Practice and Theory of Creative Writing, 11*(2), 208–227.

Moorman, H. (2006). Backing into ekphrasis: Reading and writing poetry about visual art. *English Journal, 96*(1), 46–53.

Mouawad, W. (2003). *Incendies.* Montréal, QC: Leméac.

Nussbaum, M. C. (1998). The narrative imagination. In N. C. Nussbaum, *Cultivating humanity: A classical defense of reform in liberal education* (pp. 85–112). Cambridge, MA: Harvard University Press.

Pantaleo, S. (2013). Revisiting Rosenblatt's aesthetic response through *The Arrival*. *Australian Journal of Language and Literacy, 36*(3), 125–134.

Probst, R. E. (1990). *Literature as exploration* and the classroom. In E. J. Farrell & J. R. Squire (Eds.), *Transactions with literature: A fifty-year perspective*. Urbana, IL: National Council of Teachers of English.

Purves, A. & Rippere, V. (1968). Elements of writing about a literary work: A study of response to literature. Urbana, IL: National Council of Teachers of English.

Ricoeur, P. (1981). *Hermeneutics and the human sciences: Essays on language, action and interpretation* (J. Thompson trans.). Cambridge, MA: Cambridge University Press, and Paris, France: Éditions de la Maison des Sciences de l'Homme.

Ricoeur, P. (1992). *Oneself as another*. Chicago, IL: Chicago University Press.

Rosenblatt, L. M. (1978). The reader, the text, the poem: The transactional theory of the literary work. Carbondale and Edwardsville, IL: Southern Illinois University Press.

Rosenblatt, L. M. (1994/2005). The transactional theory of reading and writing. In R. B. Ruddell, M. R. Ruddell, & H. Singer (Eds.), *Theoretical Models and Processes of Reading* (4th edition) (pp. 1057–1092). Republished in Rosenblatt, L. M. (2005). *Making meaning with texts: Selected essays* (pp. 1–37). Portsmouth, NH: Heinemann.

Rowsell, J. (2014). Toward a phenomenology of contemporary reading. *Australian Journal of Language and Literacy, 37*(2), 117–126.

Sager Eidt, L. M. (2008). *Writing and filming the painting: Ekphrasis in literature and film*. Amsterdam, The Netherlands, and New York, NY: Rodopi.

Sarroub, L. K. & Pernicek, T. (2016). Boys, books, and boredom: A case of three high school boys and their encounters with literacy. *Reading & Writing Quarterly, 32*(1), pp. 27–55.

Swanger, D. (2013). Notes on empathy in poetry. In B. White & T. Costantino (Eds.), *Aesthetics, Empathy and Education* (pp. 117–131). New York, NY: Peter Lang.

Van Manen, M. (1990). *Researching lived experience: Human science for an action sensitive pedagogy*. London, ON: Althouse Press.

Van Manen, M. (2014). *Phenomenology of practice: Meaning-giving methods in phenomenological research and writing*. Walnut Creek, CA: Left Coast Press.

White, B. (1998). Aesthetigrams: Mapping aesthetic experiences. *Studies in Art Education, 39*(4), 321–335.

White, B. (2007). Aesthetic encounters: Contributions to teacher education. *International Journal of Education & the Arts, 8*(17), 1–28.

White, B. (2013). Pay attention, pay attention, pay attention. In B. White & T. Costantino (Eds.), *Aesthetics, Empathy and Education* (pp. 99–116). New York, NY: Peter Lang.

White, B. & Frois, J. P. (2013). Words for artworks: The aesthetics of meaning making. *International Journal of Art & Design Education, 32*(1), 109–123.

White, B. (2014). Student generated art criticism. *The Canadian Review of Art Education, 41*(1), 32–55.

Wiebe, S. (2013). Aesthetic/empathetic punctures through poetry. In B. White & T. Costantino (Eds.), *Aesthetics, Empathy and Education* (pp. 135–150). New York, NY: Peter Lang.

CHAPTER FIVE

Applications with CEGEP (18–20-Year-Old) Students

AMÉLIE LEMIEUX

We saw in Chapter 4 that the play and film *Incendies* were used in a study with high school students. In this chapter, I present the applications of aesthetigram research with post-secondary college (CEGEP) students, who are between 18 and 20 years old.

Acknowledgement: I would like to thank the Social Sciences and Humanities Research Council of Canada for supporting the research presented in this chapter. This chapter was translated in English by permission of Revue de Recherches en Littératie Médiatique Multimodale (R2LMM), who holds the French rights.

—Amélie Lemieux

RESEARCH PROBLEM AND CONTEXT

Recent studies focusing on students' subjectivities when interpreting texts have been oriented towards reader phenomenology (Lemieux, 2015; Lemieux & Lacelle, 2016; Lewkowich, 2015, 2016a, 2016b; Pantaleo, 2013; Sauvaire, 2013, 2015). Congruently, a report from the Quebec Ministry of Education has established that teachers had difficulty adopting teaching strategies that (1) stimulated readers' reactions to text, (2) called for readers' opinions when they read, and (3) allowed for alternative critiquing of the narrative through the use of "mental images" (Brehm, 2008; Lewkowich, 2015, 2016a, 2016b). Most literature teachers still prefer using traditional methods (Pierce, 1977; Todorov, 1982), a lot of which have been discussed in a recent special issue published by R2LMM. This chapter continues this discussion, and suggests an alternative to teaching strategies that are based on traditional reading tests. I stress the importance of valorizing readers' conscience (Lewkowich, 2015, 2016a, 2016b; Iftody, Sumara, & Davis, 2006; Sumara, Luce-Kapler, & Iftody, 2008) through the images they invoke as they read (Brehm, 2008; Lacelle & Langlade, 2007; Langlade, 2006, 2008, 2013). Largely influenced by the works of Lacelle (2009, 2012), I adopt, for the potential and the conclusive effects of literature teaching through transwritings (Gaudreault & Groensteen, 1998), attention to adapted, multimodal versions of monomodal narratives. In concert with Larrivé's (2014) work, I examine the impact of literary experiences in alternate forms by seeking answers to the following question: Might a film adaptation generate other forms of comprehension in students? If this proves to be true, what traces of such comprehension might be available to the researcher and teacher so that they could observe students' reactions to the monomodal and multimodal versions of the same narrative? Globally speaking, how might we know if these traces initiate meaning-making in the reader (Ivey & Johnston, 2013, 2015a, 2015b; Lysaker & Miller, 2013) who is subsequently a viewer?

CONCEPTUAL FRAMEWORK

This study also builds on the works of the LLA Creatis Lab (Toulouse University-Jean Jaurès) and that of other French researchers and theorists (Fourtanier, Langlade & Mazauric, 2006; Lacelle & Langlade, 2008; Langlade, 2006). Thus, my research is epistemologically based on empirical research that shed light on important aspects of the reader, such as Langlade's (2006) typology of fictional activity and Sauvaire's (2013) model of interpretive reading strategies in reception contexts. In essence, this study highlights reader subjectivity through the lens of phenomenology (Ricoeur, 1981, 1992; Van Manen, 2014; Merleau-Ponty, 1962) to unveil the plural reactive dimensions of the person who reads the text and watches the film. In this chapter, focusing on reception, I present a case study of the reactions of a CEGEP student, as documented in her aesthetigrams (Lemieux, 2015; Frois & White, 2013; White, 1998, 2007, 2011, 2013, 2014). With this teaching and research strategy, as we discussed in Chapter 3, students have the chance to mobilize subjective resources (Sauvaire, 2013) and filter their reactions through writing and structured organising of their reactions. The aesthetigram exercise is conducted with the sole aim of offering opportunities to visually record interactions with text in both its modal (original printed text) and multimodal form (its film adaptation). The written reactions of Olivia, a CEGEP student, were collected in the context of her course on Quebec literature. Her results are, overall, representative of that of her peers. Similarly to Pantaleo's (2013) approach, I chose this student who participated in a relatively large study (N = 50) in order to demonstrate the range and potential of aesthetigram-making in relation to self-exploration (White, 2013) research applications (Lemieux, 2015; White, 2007, 2014), and teaching (White, 1998, 2011; White and Tompkins, 2005). I present reading also as a multimodal act (we have argued this elsewhere in Lemieux & Lacelle, in press), where the reader summons a series of mental images and impressions that are imperative to the development of their narrative imagination (Lysaker & Miller, 2013; Nussbaum, 1998) and their desires (Lewkowich, 2015).

Reactions to the written and film narrative, two distinct but related forms, embody reader experiences, including aesthetic reading experiences (Rosenblatt, 1978). Similarly, Sumara, (1998) talks about the importance of the *vécu* [self-awareness] in the reading act, showing how this aspect dictates reading conditions and embodiment of the narrative through reading. In other words, the reader perceives himself as being part of the narrative. This perspective, of primary concern in the study of reader subjectivity, is in line with the results found by Ivey and Johnston (2015a), who posited that reader engagement depends on the development of social imagination through his encounters with fictional characters (Similar theories have been advanced by Bogdan, 1992; Nussbaum, 1998; and Sumara, Luce-Kapler & Iftody, 2008) and his ability to articulate his metacognitive interactions with fictional characters (Iftody, Sumara, & Davis, 2006; Lacelle & Langlade, 2007; Langlade, 2006; Sumara, Luce-Kapler & Iftody, 2008). Building on this, Lysaker and Miller (2013) maintain that "relationships with others, and the talk that constructs and surrounds those relationships, provide experiences that afford the development of social imagination … reading is one of those relational experiences." (p. 150)

Ivey and Johnston (2013) demonstrated that a reader's social imagination depends on his reading engagement. Engaged reading implies, according to these authors, socio-emotional, moral, and ethical dimensions. Lysaker and Miller (2013) add that students can "think, feel, imagine and dream with the characters in books and explore possible selves by taking on the positions of others as their own." (p. 150) This statement echoes the essential guidelines of the subject-reader theory (Langlade, 2006), where the reader develops fictional activity through similar strategies. Lysaker and Miller (2013) stipulate that one's capacity to articulate multiple reading interpretations is a tangible proof of reader engagement. In that sense, the researchers show that a student's flexible cognition is essentially metacognitive. It can be articulated by means of imaginations, reactions, and feelings towards the "Other," who is represented by fictional characters. These important dialogic traces lead to inferences that are necessary to readers' engagement (Lysaker & Miller, 2013, p. 167). The aesthetigram exercise (White, 1998;

Lemieux, 2015) moves in that direction and suggests metacognitives and meta-linguistic avenues to reader engagement, as detailed by Lysaker and Miller (2013).

A film adaptation of a written book, which has been theorised as an "inter-modal transmodalisation" (Genette, 1992) or a "transmediatic transwriting" (Gaudreault & Groensteen, 1998), serves as a complement to reader engagement. Many studies have shown that film, when used in classrooms, bolsters engagement (Lacelle, 2009; Purves, Rogers & Soter, 1990). Although each film adaptation calls for, in itself, new readings of the piece, reading and viewing experiences offer rich possibilities to teach artworks like books and films. Paying attention to students' reactions in reading and viewing situations is to recognize the legitimacy of form and the mutuality of films and literature (Purves, Rogers, & Soter, 1990). Class-room activities provide opportunities to study such reactions. This study demon-strates this possibility.

METHODOLOGY

This research was conducted in Montreal, in fall 2014, with two groups of 25 students ($N = 50$), enrolled in an international post-secondary programme (CEGEP) leading to university studies. The students had enrolled in a Quebec literature course as part of their degree completion requirements. The research project had first been discussed with Mary,[1] their French teacher, over four preliminary meet-ings. Our first objective was to merge teaching and research in order to follow the course and program requirements. The merger was realized through the imple-mentation of a comparative dialectic table, which resulted in a longer student essay. This part was evaluated by the teacher as part of the students' grades on émigré Quebec literature. Together, we developed a portfolio that included the following documents: (1) a pre-test highlighting readers' profiles, (2) a reading questionnaire, (3) two aesthetigrams in relation to the reading and viewing of the *Letter to the Son*, with accompanying commentary, (4) two ekphrastic writing pieces as extensions of the first and second aesthetigrams, (5) the comparative dialectic table, and (6) a post-test on students' reactions to the project.

Mary developed a criterion-based evaluation scheme (Durant & Chouinard, 2012) and rubrics. She chose to evaluate the following work, for a total of 15% of students' final grade.

(1) The comparative dialectic table worth 5% (70% for content, 30% for language).
(2) A piece chosen by the student (5%), from either: the reading question-naire, two aesthetigrams and their justifications, or the ekphrasis writings and their justifications.
(3) The overall portfolio (rigour, presentation, completeness) (5%).

The research project took place over ten (10) hours of class and five (5) additional hours to read the play at home and complete the portfolio exercises that were not finished during classroom time. Most students were able to do the assignments during class time. I present below a participant's aesthetigrams, accompanying commentary, and ekphrastic writing. The analysis is phenomenological (Butler-Kisber, 2010; van Manen, 1990), and is entirely based on the student's reactions in relation to the text and film.

AESTHETIGRAMS

The aesthetigram-making process is both multi-dimensional and subjective. In this study, the aesthetigram concept had been introduced to students during the first class of the project in the fall 2014. In the preliminary phase, I conceived and visually demonstrated the steps for making an aesthetigram on PowerPoint. I gave the presentation in class, and the slides were uploaded on Moodle for student reference. The categories of reactions of the aesthetigram were adapted from White's (2011) strategy, which was originally developed in the context of viewing visual art. I adapted these categories for the reading of written narratives and the viewing of films. I asked students to react to scene 37 (Letter to the Son) in the play, and to its corresponding scene in the film. The same steps as those listed in Chapter 3 were followed during the process. The entirety of *Incendies* was shown in class, but I replayed the scene so that students could complete their list of reactions in real time. In order to write their reactions properly, students asked me to replay the scene, as the flow of the scene was relatively fast (approximately 2 minutes) in comparison to the writing time available for their reactions to the written narrative. Then too, as the narrative is read differently depending on reading pace, reactions to the text were collected at irregular intervals (for reasons later described).

EKPHRASTIC WRITING

Mary and I gave students directions for ekphrastic writing in relation to their aesthetigrams. They had an hour to write a poem, short story, or genre of their choice (a letter, for instance). Each written production was accompanied by commentary, outlining the reasons why they chose a particular genre and the reflections on their reading-viewing-writing experiences. Students could write as much as they pleased. The objective was to gather students' metacognitive experiences and to reproduce them in writing.

POWER OF THE NARRATIVES

Since the play and the film share essentially the same story, and that, in this chapter, I do not investigate the differences between the two modalities, I looked at students' reactions when they "react [ed] to text in all of its forms." With Mary's advice, I chose Scene 37 (as in Chapter 3) because this scene was present in both modalities. The scene depicts various intimate layers of human complexity. It depicts the journey of a mother who suffered because of her son, who was guilty of raping her. But there was also joy in the reunion because he was her long-lost son. The *Letter to the Son* reveals the narrative's climax. That is, Nihad had raped his mother when she was a prison inmate. I have previously noted (in Chapter 3 and in Lemieux, 2015) that this scene stimulated vivid reactions in students, due to the emotional, dualistic, and poignant nature of the written and film narrative.

AESTHETIGRAMS AND ANALYSIS

One of the objectives of this chapter is to show the potential of aesthetigrams as research and teaching tools.

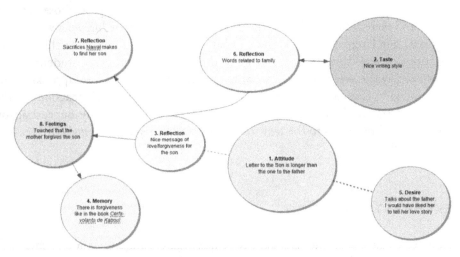

Fig 5.1. Aesthetigram based on Olivia's reactions to the Letter to the Son in the play.
Source: Author's dissertation data.

Because aesthetigrams allow participants to reflect on their own reactions and, thus, on the intricacies of their reception (Frois & White, 2013; Lemieux, 2015), it seems reasonable that Olivia's observations point to the reflections category, even though she admitted that that response was the way she usually reacts: "My reactions are separated into six categories, including the reflection category that has more elements ... I reflect a lot on the literary and cinematographic artworks after reading or seeing them." Thus, Olivia expressed a critical distance towards the book when she identified the number of reactions linked to this category.

Olivia also manifests her inter-textual associative knowledge through the connections she made with Khaled Hosseini's novel *Les Cerfs-Volants de Kaboul*. This inter-textual reference is logically organised in her aesthetigram, and is linked to her other structured reactions:

> I placed my most important reaction in the middle, and I linked most elements to it. On the bottom left, I placed everything linked to the letter's content and its aesthetics. It was related to my reading to another book, *Les Cerfs-volants de Kaboul*. In the latter novel, the main character saw his friend being raped, but he did not intervene to save him. He apologizes through a letter as well.

As readers of her aesthetigram, we can follow her manner of operation, notably when it comes to the pragmatic articulation of her reactions. Inter-textually speaking, and according to the participant, the common element between both narratives is the rape and the apology through the means of a letter. This association certainly depicts a meta-reflection, not only on *Incendies*, but also on potential links with other narratives of similar nature. These are part of Olivia's cultural and literary repertoire.

Olivia provided meta-linguistic reflections: "I reflected on linguistic aspects, like on the lexical field and stylistic elements," and her desires as a reader: "I added one of my 'desire' reactions regarding what I would have liked to find in the letter." This last reflection reminds us of the theory of "reading as desire" (Lewkowich, 2015, 2016a, 2016b), based on the premise that the reader, according to a Freudian psychoanalytic perspective, sees that the narrative mirrors what can be seen, read, and perceived. Olivia's "desire" can be interpreted as her contribution to the narrative (Sumara, 1998). That is, even if her desire was not entirely materialized in the play, her reflection was unquestionably part of her transaction with the narrative. Such a transaction can only be completed by the reader (Barthes, 1984; Rosenblatt, 1978).

There were three (3) moments of reflections, and other reactions were equitably divided among other categories (taste, attitude, desire, memory, and feelings). From these results, we can see that the participant reacted primarily in terms of attitude. That moment, however, and the ones that followed, led to important reflexive pauses that explain the relationship between form and content, and what they contributed to each other.

EKPHRASTIC WRITING, BUILDING ON THE FIRST AESTHETIGRAM

Olivia wrote the following letter to expand on her reactions located in her first aesthetigram:

> By writing this letter, my son, I seek to express the eternal love I have for my exceptional son, born from the love your father and I had for each other. Just like me, you were a war victim, this war that changed us, that separated us one from another and through which we met each other under unusual circumstances of a mother loving her son. I am trying to show you, through these kind words and all these images, that love will always win over hate. And no matter all that we have been through, I am really happy that we met each other. My dear son, the life that awaits you will not be an easy one, but because you were born out of love, just like your brother and sister, a path will open up.

Olivia's Comments: I decided to write a letter, because poems and prose limit my creativity and imagination. Indeed, there is a whole creative process (rhymes, metaphors, poem meaning) that *constrains* me from being creative when I write. I would rather write a narrative that encompasses all my thoughts precisely and rapidly, without *feeling stressed* about integrating elements of style. I would rather write without these constraints.

In her commentary, Olivia sees poetic writing as a limit or a constraint to her imagination. It seems impossible to unpack the stereotypes from these lines that Olivia has towards traditional poems (perhaps, all poems are composed of Alexandrines,

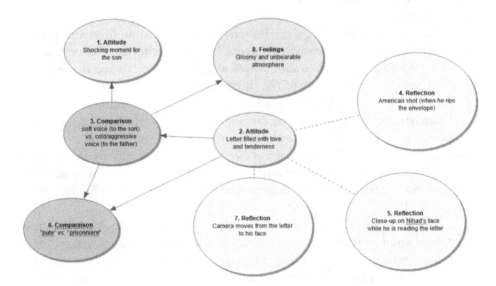

Fig 5.2. Aesthetigram based on Olivia's reactions to the *Letter to the Son* (film version).
Source: Author's dissertation data.

whose form is very square and rhymed). Let us not forget, however, that the letter also has a precise genre, etiquette, and codes. Further evidence suggests why Olivia chose the letter as genre, like her desire to personify her writing: "In my writing, I used Nawal's voice, because it was easier to express the love she displayed in her letter." This personification enabled Olivia to show the themes that emerged from her first aesthetigram. She was able to express, through her writing, affective themes: "In this piece, I gave priority to the theme of love, because it's the one that was most evident". All in all, despite the participant's initial resistance to include stylistic elements in her writing, she still gave it a try so that she could personalise her letter: "I added a few stylistic devices like metaphor, comparison, personifications, because Nawal was a smart and respectable woman so, in her image, I did include some." In sum, Olivia's writing production articulates three main areas: a need to express form and genre, a need to communicate content intricacies, but also to create a bridge between form and content.

OLIVIA'S COMMENTARY ON HER AESTHETIGRAM

First, I placed the most important element in the center. From there, I could identify two comparisons that were as important: one on content of the letter (how Nawal signed her name at the end of the letter) and the other on her tone of voice. Then, in that reaction, where she speaks coldly to the father, but also speaks with a warm voice to the son (where he learns that he impregnated his mother by raping her) represents a shocking moment in his life that just changed forever. I linked reactions 1 and 3 together. From there, I felt the atmosphere becoming gloomy and unbearable. The close-up on Nihad's face when he was reading the letter emphasized his facial expressions, which accentuated the dramatic effects in the scene. The reflections I had when viewing the scene of the film were my observations building on cinema codes, like the angles and shots that altered the effects of the scene. Even if these reactions were not directly linked to feelings, attitudes or comparisons, they were as important to make the scene as dramatic as it was.

I reproduced the commentary in its entirety, as Olivia wrote it in her portfolio, because the use of transition words and connectives indicate clearly her thought development and progressive aesthetigram construction. First, Olivia explained that she established relevant links between content and tone (as heard and not imagined, because of the film's modality). Nawal's tone, perceived as cold, marks a love contrast for the son, who is also the rapist. This tension, really palpable in the actors' play, was a cathartic experience for the participant, as she wrote in her reactions. Olivia observed, regarding the film's multimodal form and its cathartic effects: "The *close-up* on Nihad's face when he was reading the letter emphasized his facial expressions, which accentuated the *dramatic effects* in the scene." The union of form and content as well as the influence of form *on* content are explicit in her explanations. The student added, on the effects of form on content: "Even if these reactions were not directly linked to feelings, attitudes or comparisons, they were as important to make the scene as dramatic as it was." Overall, Olivia's reactions towards the same scene (but this time, its film version) present all the important elements of the play as adapted. The multimodal performance provoked a cathartic effect in the participant who, in turn, recognized that the codes were at the origins of this ethos.

Olivia noted two comparative moments in her aesthetigram. Indeed, she noted important contrasts in the binary themes of the narrative (e.g., "whore" vs. "prisoner"; Nawal's warm tone towards the son and her cold tone when addressing the rapist). One of the most important findings of this study is that the aforementioned binary moments, intensified by the film's multimodality, were subsequently seen by the student who had not, at first, noticed them. We think that the tone could not have been perceived in its monomodal version, or perhaps during a brief stimulation of mental images (Langlade, 2006), because the tone was not imposed or performed in the book and therefore Olivia did not initially express reactions towards it. These three reflective moments suggest observations that were directed towards form (e.g., mention of camera shots or movements) and that influenced the perception of content. Finally, moments of attitude (2) and feelings (1) were linked to affective effects related to the participant's reception of the film.

OLIVIA'S CREATIVE WRITING BASED ON HER SECOND AESTHETIGRAM

> From this letter you left me, mother, an abyssal gap formed throughout my life was finally filled, but another one formed again. Yes, mother, I felt all the love you had for me. Yes, mother, I know that you forgave me, but guilt is eating me alive. Why did this happen to us? Why is life so unfair? Why didn't I recognize you in prison or at the pool? Even if I am blessed by having found you, I don't know what to do nor think. What should I do now, mom?

In her commentary, Olivia suggested a reflection once again based on form and the benefits of the letter as a suitable genre for her: "I once again wrote a letter, because this genre does not limit me in my writing." Just as in her first ekphrastic writing, Olivia explained that the letter, as genre, has the potential to personify and personalize affect: "In this production, I gave priority to the shocking revelation that this letter had on Nihad, and I made him the narrator of the letter, because he was best suited to tell this overwhelming scene." Olivia also justified her systematic use of interrogatives: "I used a lot of question marks to show the son's incomprehension in face of this situation. Nihad asks his mother questions to show that he is confused and disturbed after having read the truth on his family." Through her awareness of connections between form and content, and through her creative writing, Olivia was able to make meaning of her aesthetigram.

LIMITATIONS

The post-secondary context has its complexities in terms of class attendance. Similar to university settings, CEGEP rules and syllabi dictate that students' in-class presence is mandatory. But given the flexible school schedules and heavier workload than secondary school ones, several participants did not respect these rules. In consequence, they had to catch up by completing the portfolio documents at home. Of the fifty participants, some of them could not hand in all documents at the expected time. This discrepancy kept the teacher from completing evaluations of all portfolio documents. Thus, we had to develop an evaluation plan so that students would complete the course. From an ethical perspective, 15% of students' total grade (described earlier) was reasonable, according to the REB, and we respected that guideline. I felt it was relevant, in that vein, to present Olivia's perspective in order to spark future research.

This chapter has presented a case study. In future studies, I will have opportunities to amass a more global portrait of readers' reactions. In the meantime, I hope that my presentation of a single portrait may suggest new avenues for research for colleagues working in reading studies and literature pedagogy.

CONCLUSION

In this chapter, I have described how aesthetigrams enabled the student to situate her moments of reaction in reading and viewing contexts. Even though each aesthetigram presented moments of reaction that were different, depending on the reading or viewing mode, we observed recurring dispositions and results in both aesthetigrams and its effects. For instance, visual maps helped the participant articulate links between form and content, regardless of the modality. In both cases, Olivia's transaction (Rosenblatt, 1978) with the narrative shows comparisons and differentiations according to (1) the moment of reaction, and (2) the medium (multimodal or monomodal/printed). Therefore, I conclude that aesthetigrams can be useful in fine tuning participants' reactions and can help them in meaning making when reading and viewing artworks.

When it comes to students' productions, while I have found in the larger study that ekphrastic writing helps students explore new creative endeavours, I noticed that poetic writing is not suitable for all students. Thus, I recognized the necessity to let students choose their writing genre. In Olivia's case, the letter proved to be an ideal tool to express reactive situations after reading and viewing the same scene. Her reflections on form and content show the impact of aesthetigrams on creative writing, in that this first step enabled construction of a framework for ensuing writing. It is essential that students feel empowered through their actions and reactions to literature in order to develop their reading engagement. In that sense, this study offers epistemological and methodological avenues that highlight readers' subjectivities. We encourage researchers to observe, in future works, reactions to other modalities, including kinaesthetic modalities implying more "embodied" (Sumara, 1998) transactions as experienced through touch and interactive reading.

NOTE

1. Mary is a pseudonym.

REFERENCES

Barthes, R. (1984). La mort de l'auteur. In *Le bruissement de la langue. Essais critiques IV*. Paris: Seuil.

Bogdan, D. (1992). *Re-education the imagination: Towards a poetics, politics, and pedagogy of literary engagement*. Portsmouth: Heinemann.

Brehm, S. (2008). Le rôle de l'imaginaire dans le processus de référenciation. *Figura, 20*, 31–44.

Butler-Kisber, L. (2010). *Interpretive Inquiry*. London: Sage.

Durand, M.-J. & Chouinard, R. (2012). *L'évaluation des apprentissages: De la planification de la démarche à la communication des résultats*. Montréal: Marcel Didier.

Fourtanier, M.-J., Langlade, G., & Mazauric C. (2006). Dispositifs de lecture et formation des lecteurs. Proceedings of the 7th Annual Meeting of «chercheurs en didactique de la littérature» Montpellier: Montpellier University.

Frois, J. P. & White, B. (2013). Words for artworks: The aesthetics of meaning making. *International Journal of Art & Design Education, 32*(1), 109–125.

Gaudreault, A. & Groensteen, T. (Eds.) (1998). La transécriture: Pour une théorie de l'adaptation. Littérature, cinéma, bande dessinée, théâtre, clip. Québec: Nota Bene.

Genette, G. (1992). *Palimpsestes*. Paris: Seuil.

Iftody, T., Sumara, D. J., et Davis, B. (2006). Consciousness and the literary engagement: Toward a bio-cultural theory of reading and learning. *Language and Literacy, 8*(1), 1–24.

Ivey, G. & Johnston, P. H. (2013). Engagement with young adult literature: Outcomes and processes. *Reading Research Quarterly, 48*(3), 255–275.

Ivey, G. & Johnston, P. H. (2015a). *Persistence of the experience of engaged reading*. Paper presented at the annual conference of the Literacy Research Association. Carlsbad, CA, December 2015.

Ivey, G. & Johnston, P. H. (2015b). Engaged reading as a collaborative transformative practice. *Journal of Literacy Research, 47*(3), 297–327.

Lacelle, N. (2009). *Modèle de lecture-spectature, à l'intention didactique, de l'œuvre littéraire et de son adaptation filmique*, (unpublished doctoral thesis). Université du Québec à Montréal.

Lacelle, N. (2012). Des propositions d'enseignement de la lecture littéraire et filmique pour fonder une didactique de la lecture multimodale. In Lebrun, M., Lacelle, N. & J.-F. Boutin (Eds.). *La littératie médiatique multimodale: De nouvelles approches en lecture-écriture à l'école et hors de l'école* (pp. 171–187). Québec: Presses de l'Université du Québec.

Lacelle, N. & Langlade, G. (2007). Former des lecteurs/spectateurs par la lecture subjective des œuvres. In J.-L. Dufays, *Enseigner et apprendre la littérature aujourd'hui pour quoi faire?* (pp. 55–65). Louvain-la-Neuve: Presses Universitaires de Louvain.

Langlade, G. (2006). L'activité fictionnalisante du lecteur. Dans M. Braud, B. Laville, et B. Louichon (Eds.). *Les enseignements de la fiction* (pp. 163–176). Bordeaux: PUB.

Langlade, G. (2008). Activité fictionnalisante du lecteur et dispositif de l'imaginaire. *Figura, 20*, 45–65.

Langlade, G. (2013). Chartreuse(s) de Parme: D'une lecture subjective à l'autre. In N. Rannou (Ed.), *L'expérience du sujet lecteur: travaux en cours* (pp. 41–52). Grenoble: Presses de l'Université de Grenoble.

Larrivé, V. (2014). *Du bon usage du bovarysme dans la classe de français: développer l'empathie fictionnelle des élèves pour les aider à lire les récits littéraires: l'exemple du journal de personnage* (unpublished doctoral thesis). Bordeaux: Université de Bordeaux.

Lemieux, A. (2015). Think it *through*: Fostering aesthetic experiences to raise interest in literature at the high school level. *Journal of the Canadian Association for Curriculum Studies, 12*(2), 66–93. Retrieved from: http://jcacs.journals.yorku.ca/index.php/jcacs/article/view/37301/36029. Accessed June 28, 2017.

Lemieux, A. & Lacelle, N. (2016). Approches transactionnelle, subjective, et phénoménologique en didactique de la lecture. *Myriades: Revues d'études francophones, 2*(1), 14–28. Retrieved from: http://cehum.ilch.uminho.pt/myriades/static/volumes/2–2.pdf. Accessed June 28, 2017

Lemieux, A. & Lacelle, N. (under review). Mobilizing students' interpretive resources: A novel take on subjective response in the literature classroom. *Language and Literacy.*

Lewkowich, D. (2015). Transferences of teacher-casting and projections of redemptions: Teacher education, young adult literature and the psychic life of reading. *Pedagogy, Culture & Society, 23*(3), 349–368. DOI: 10.1080/14681366.2014.977808.

Lewkowich, D. (2016a). To enter the text as into a dream: Tracing the unconscious effects of reading experience. *International Journal of Research & Method in Education, 39*(1), 58–73.

Lewkowich, D. (2016b). The problem of endings in teacher education: Interpreting narratives of fictional adolescence. *International Journal of Qualitative Studies in Education, 29*(6), 745–762. DOI: 10.1080/09518398.2016.1145279.

Lysaker, J. T. & Miller, A. (2013). Engaging social imagination: The developmental work of wordless book reading. *Journal of Early Childhood Literacy, 13*(2), 147–174.

Merleau-Ponty, M. (1962). *Phenomenology of perception: An introduction.* London: Routledge.

Ministère de l'Éducation, du Loisir et du Sport (2005). *La lecture chez les élèves du secondaire: Action concertée pour le soutien à la recherche en lecture.* Report 04-01069, ISBN 2-550-43826-4.

Nussbaum, M. C. (1998). The narrative imagination. In N. C. Nussbaum, *Cultivating humanity: A classical defense of reform in liberal education* (pp. 85–112). Cambridge, MA: Harvard University Press.

Pantaleo, S. (2013). Revisiting Rosenblatt's aesthetic response through *The Arrival. Australian Journal of Language and Literacy, 36*(3), 125–134.

Peirce, C. S. (1977). *Semiotics and Significs* (revised edition by Charles Hardwick). Bloomington, IN: Indiana University Press.

Purves, A. C., Rogers, T., & Soter, A. O. (1990). *How porcupines make love II: Teaching a response-centered literature curriculum.* New York & London: Longman.

Rosenblatt, L. M. (1978). *The reader, the text, the poem: The transactional theory of the literary work.* Carbondale & Edwardsville: Southern Illinois University Press.

Ricoeur, P. (1981). *Hermeneutics and the human sciences: Essays on language, action and interpretation* (J. Thompson trans.). Cambridge, MA: Cambridge University Press, & Paris: Éditions de la Maison des Sciences de l'Homme.

Ricoeur, P. (1992). *Oneself as another.* Chicago: Chicago University Press.

Sauvaire, M. (2013). *Diversité des lectures littéraires: Comment former des sujets lecteurs divers?* (unpublished doctoral thesis). Université Laval, Québec & Université Toulouse Le Mirail, Toulouse.

Sauvaire, M. (2015). Diversité des sujets lecteurs dans l'enseignement de la lecture littéraire. *Éducation et didactique, 9*(2), 107–117.

Sumara, D. J. (1998). Fictionalizing acts: Reading and the making of identity. *Theory into practice, 37*(3), 203–210.

Sumara, D. J., Luce-Kapler, R., & Iftody, T. (2008). Educating consciousness through literary experiences. *Educational Philosophy and Theory, 40*(1), 228–241.

Todorov, T. (1982). *Symbolism and Interpretation*, trans. Catherine Porter. Ithaca: Cornell University Press.

Van Manen, M. (2014). *Phenomenology of practice: Meaning-giving methods in phenomenological research and writing.* Walnut Creek, CA: Left Coast Press.

White, B. (1998). Aesthetigrams: Mapping aesthetic experiences. *Studies in Art Education, 39*(40), 321–335.

White, B. (2007). Aesthetic encounters: Contributions to teacher education. *International Journal of Education & the Arts, 8*(17), 1–28.

White, B. (2011). Private perceptions, public reflections: Aesthetic encounters as vehicles for shared meaning making. *International Journal of Education & the Arts, 12* (LAI 2), 1–26.

White, B. (2013). Pay attention, pay attention, pay attention. In B. White & T. Costantino (Eds.), *Aesthetics, Empathy and Education* (pp. 99–116). New York, NY: Peter Lang.

White, B. (2014). Student generated art criticism. *The Canadian Review of Art Education, 41*(1), 32–55.

White, B. & Tompkins, S. (2005). Doing aesthetics to facilitate meaning-making. *Arts and Learning Research Journal, 21*(1), 1–36.

Introduction

Other Applications

In this final section, we look at applications of the aesthetigram strategy within alternative settings. That is, while the aesthetigram strategy was initially intended for use within a formal university class where the focus was on learning in relation to interactions with artworks, we became interested in seeing how it might be adapted elsewhere. Amélie began that adaptation process with her work in litera- ture classes, at both secondary and post-secondary levels. These exercises were still within the framework of formal education. We thought it would be interesting to see what we could do within informal settings. This unit introduces two such settings. One is a poetry workshop. The other, Chapter 7, features an after-school philosophy-for-childen (P4C) workshop.

CHAPTER SIX

The Poetry Workshop

BOYD WHITE

Participants in the poetry workshop were all members of an informal local poetry-writing group who meet regularly. Six members of the group, five women and one man, agreed to experiment with an ekphrastic exercise.

Contemporary ekphrasis-inspired poetry usually focuses on an artwork, often a painting or photograph, and considers it through a variety of possible stances—dialogic, descriptive, philosophic, and so forth. It might or might not describe parts of the artwork, and indeed the artwork need not even physically exist except in the imagination of the poet. Thus the poem is not an attempt to transfer an artwork from visual image into word. It is not a copy. Rather, the poem is a creative, act of imagination. This was the challenge I set for the workshop.

Being a small group, we were able to meet in a quiet room at a local library. We all sat around one table. I began with a warm-up exercise.

We looked at a Sally Mann black and white photograph called *Candy cigarette*, although I initially hid the title of the work. The image shows a young girl, perhaps as old as 12, flaunting what looks to be a real cigarette. She is photographed from the waist up, wearing a summer dress. She has striking long blond hair that frames her face and shoulders. The child has a self-composed, contemplative expression on her face. Her dark eyes stare into the camera. If we look at the face alone, we might think she is quite a bit older than she actually is. The portrait is in sharp focus. All the detail is crisp. In front of the child (to our right) is another, younger child with her back to us, in a dark dress, hands on her hips. She is not in as sharp focus, and the detail is less pronounced. And in the background, upper left, is a somewhat fuzzy image of what looks to be another child on a pair of stilts. The sex of that child is indeterminate. All we see is the child's back in a long T-shirt. As a group we studied the photograph and speculated on its meaning. After a while I told the group the title of the photograph. This changed people's interpretations quite a bit. I added some contextual detail about Sally Mann's work—the fact that she used to pose her children in somewhat theatrical fashion, sometimes nude when they were pre-pubescent. This information added another layer to the group's interpretations. In all, we spent around 20 minutes looking at and commenting on the photograph. Then I began the main exercise.

I started by introducing the concept of aesthetigrams and their purpose—to assist us in becoming aware of our patterns of response to generally aesthetically endowed objects. I also showed a couple of examples of computer-generated aesthetigrams. But I thought the group would prefer a more dialogic approach to the exercise, so I did not ask them to bring computers, (which tend to encourage more isolated activity, even within a group setting).

Then I showed them another black and white photograph, John Dugdale's *The artist's mother*. In addition to an $8^{1/2}$ × 11 inch hard copy of an image that we passed around, I also brought my laptop computer to our gathering so participants could compare the electronic version to a printout. I also brought materials to assist in the making of aesthetigrams—large sheets of heavy white paper, post-it notes, coloured markers. We regularly use these methods in aesthetigram-making.

To begin, I asked them to look at the image, without talking, and to use the post-it notes to record in a few words whatever reactions they had to the image, one reaction per post-it. I asked them to number their reactions as they proceeded. After about 15 minutes most in the group had stopped taking notes, or they slowed down and made only occasional notes, apparently afterthoughts. One or two were still intently scribbling on their post-it pads. Then I invited the group to share their observations. During the ensuing discussion I said that if they wanted to add to their pile of post-its at this point, they should do so. The conversation was thoughtful and respectful of one another's observations. There was a fair amount of consensus as to the meaning of the work—of impending adult challenges.

Then I handed around to each participant the list of categories of possible experiential moments (as shown in Chapter 3) and explained that for each post-it notation there was likely to be a category into which they could slot that reaction. They took considerable time rereading their notes and trying to allocate each one to an appropriate category. I suggested they use the coloured markers to help identify reactions that seemed to belong to the same category. For example, if a participant had several perception-oriented moments, (such as various textures in hair, clothing, and skin, which several people commented on) she could use a single colour, perhaps a dot or other mark at the top of the post-it note. A memory-oriented reaction would require a different colour, and so on. Once the participants had addressed all their individual notes and identified categories, I asked them to arrange their post-its on their own large sheet of paper in such a way that we could all see the progression of their responses. Each person's "map" was in some respects different from everyone else's. About half an hour went by while people decided on the placement of their post-its. I also suggested that people could draw arrows from one post-it (experiential moment) to another if they felt that one reaction prompted another. Alternatively, some reactions could have appeared unrelated to others, in which case no arrows would be necessary. This does not mean that the moment was not linked to the others. It would have been part of the temporal sequence after all, but the response may seem to have had no apparent connection to the rest. I also asked the participants to be aware of whether a particular category or categories predominated. I reminded them that this would suggest a certain tendency in one's patterns of meaning making. They looked at each other's aesthetigrams, made comments and asked questions wherever that seemed appropriate. See Figure 6.1.

By this time about an hour and a half had gone by. I suggested that the participants use their aesthetigrams as a springboard for the writing of a poem. Most of the group wanted some reflection time for the poetry writing, so we decided that they could email their poems and any further work on their aesthetigrams (in the form of scanned images). After a break, we moved on to a second activity, but here I will limit discussion to the aesthetigram one.

Here is an example from one participant, Penny. It is also her work in Figure 6.1 below.

Instead of the usual circles and ovals that most of my students have used in the past, Penny decided to use a slightly different mapping strategy. (The software provides a number of different options.)

In Penny's case she concentrated on four categories—interpretation, perception, feelings, and comparison. The mapping option that Penny chose automatically produces four branches, as in Figure 6.2, below. So perhaps the pre-established configuration dictated her limit of categories. Within those four categories Penny itemized details such as "vine-like patterns of veins" in the perception category or "return of the prodigal?" in the comparison category. That moment could also have been recorded within the interpretive category as a co-intended moment. But with the constraints of the mapping strategy that Penny chose, this would have been hard to illustrate. Similarly, in her interpretive corner, Penny wrote, "What intimacy!" Certainly that's a reasonable interpretation. The photograph does capture that intimacy. It also suggests an affective response. But again, with her map that would have been difficult to record unless she were to have repeated the phrase within that quadrant (lower right). Penny colour-coded her viewer/context/object emphases. They indicate a fairly balanced interaction, with somewhat less focus on the viewer. Penny emailed me her map, along with the following poem.

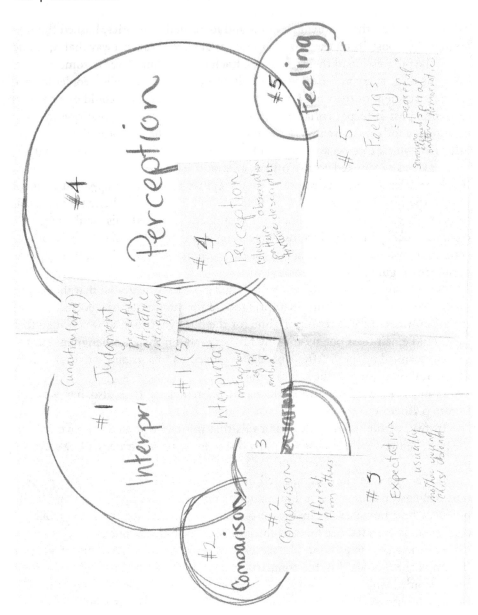

Fig 6.1. Penny's Initial "Post-It" Aesthetigram.

Source: Penny created.

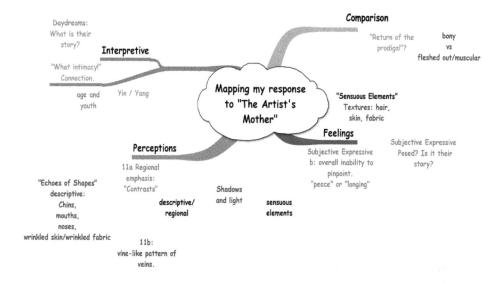

Key:
Viewer
Context
Object

Fig 6.2. Penny's Map.
Source: Penny created.

Once my hand,
strong and lithe,
spanned
my son's back.

Now arthritic fingers
clasp him to me;
my hand can't even
cover his shoulder.

Today his head
fills the space
between my cheek
and upper arm.

Once again
muscles ache, holding life;
now my heart strains against
the limitations

none of us should
bear alone.

A few weeks later she sent me another poem, not just a slight revision of the first, but one with an altogether different perspective:

Peering at Pictures

The Ikon, the dynamic dyad,
The fallen god.
Hail Mary, full of grace.

Supporting, embracing
the immanent, chthonic, erotic.
Her lunar light glows
dark and low.

Their averted eyes are united in the navel
of the whorl of the world.

In the beginning was the word
from which the fibonacci fertility unfurls.

Up and left my mind's eye travels
and gazes through
the palimpsest of memory.

Surely goodness and mercy
will follow us.

Penny's initial poem adopts the persona of the mother as she compares past and present. While the poem is definitely interpretive, it also depends on careful observation of photographed detail—her hand in comparison with his shoulder, the space his head fills. Then the poem switches to a philosophic note in the last lines.

The second poem seems to use that philosophic note as a springboard. Penny alludes to the detail without directly addressing it, with the possible exception of reference to averted eyes. Instead, Penny infers religious influence while acknowledging undertones of eros. And where the first poem ends on a suggestion of shared pain, albeit with a parallel sense of peace and acceptance, the second ends on a more active note of hope.

Looking back at Penny's aesthetigrams I wonder about the links from those to the poems, for example, to the religious allusions in the second poem. That is, where do they come from? The aesthetigrams don't say, although there is a reference to "return of the prodigal." I am left wondering if another step in the exercise might be useful. For example, in a course I teach on educational philosophy to undergraduates, one of my goals is to assist the students in the development of their identities as pre-service teachers. Using the same software that Penny used, I have students create identity maps that attempt to acknowledge their affiliations—cultural/pop cultural, linguistic, scholastic, family and friendship patterns, life style influences, and so forth. Often students are not fully aware of these influences until they are articulated in their maps. If I had started with a similar exercise with Penny's group, would contextual influences have become more pronounced in the aesthetigrams? In the next chapter Natalie describes her long-term work with a group of children and how that extensive acquaintance built trust, openness, and confidence in her participants' abilities to express themselves. I wonder what difference a longer working relationship would have made to the aesthetigrams and ensuing poems in the workshop. These are questions to be pursued in future studies. For the moment, it seems fitting to end this chapter with reflections from Penny and Erika, another participant.

Penny:

I find that my responses favour the Intrinsic/Cognitive and yet I'd like to think that I'm not so in "the periphery" that I can't respond affectively and extrinsically as well. I do find, however, that I'm wary of the sentimental in myself and others. "Wallowing," yeah—yuck!

The "possible experiential moments" stuff seemed like a grocery list, which is fine. After all, you can tell a lot about someone's diet by looking at a list. In my case, as the aesthetigram indicates, my responses are very perceptual and interpretive. What I found interesting is how that was expressed in both my collage and poem(s). I find them highly spatial on the one hand and steeped in cultural references on the other.

Anyway, it was very interesting, Boyd, to be part of this. I would have loved to have seen more of what others did. I find the best way of seeing something is to look at something else. (Can't remember who said that. Magritte?)

Erika:

Making the aesthetigrams in a group was interesting, I liked hearing what struck or moved other people, and learning from their perspective. I'm not sure if it's just the process of creating the aesthetigram or what happens when you try and pull a poem from that process, but both activities require a level of engagement with the original artwork that really stays with me. I find myself still thinking about the Dugdale piece months later, and how it fits with other images of mother and child, etc. You don't forget an artwork that you've made an aesthetigram about, and the opportunities to learn from it continue as long as you think about it.

Philosograms as Aesthetic Maps of Philosophical Inquiry

NATALIE M. FLETCHER

Can a diagram model designed to map our aesthetic experience of artwork be moulded to also capture a series of philosophical encounters? So far, this book has been exploring the aesthetigram both in concept and application, as a way of acquiring "permanent records of otherwise ephemeral experiences of mean-ing-making" (Frois & White, 2013, p. 109). Yet exposures to art share this ephem-eral quality with community-based philosophical inquiry, especially as they both bring forth a range of phenomenological dimensions that deeply affect our expe-rience but are often overlooked and thus rendered extinct in terms of meaning-making potential. In this chapter, we explore the ways in which the aesthetigram model can be adapted to represent the phenomenological experiences of engaging in collaborative philosophical inquiry, notably with children—what we are calling philosograms.[1] How can we learn about children's phenomenological experiences of thinking together through a philosophical version of an aesthetic map? We begin with an overview of the research study that resulted in philosograms within the context of the Philosophy for Children (P4C) pedagogical model, then con-sider one child's philosogram experiment, and end by surveying some of the chal-lenges and opportunities inherent in this aesthetigram adaptation. Our approach is exploratory since our research findings on philosograms are in their preliminary stages: we have no empirical claims to make as of yet. Still, we deem it important to share the process as it unfolds given what we see as an ethical and pedagogical imperative to include children's voices in accounting for their own phenomenolog-ical experiences of their educational encounters, particularly in informal learning contexts such as ours. Philosograms may prove to be one effective way of doing so, and by extension, of enriching our understanding of children's capacity for engaging in and reflecting on complex meaning-making.

EXPERIENCING PHILOSOPHY FOR CHILDREN

The P4C program was founded in the early 1970s by educational philosopher Matthew Lipman, whose original specialization in aesthetics inspired him to create a space for young people's collaborative wonderings, in hopes of enabling dialogical exchanges that would bring life to their pursuit of meaning-making. Weighed by similar concerns about children's voices, Lipman (2003) adapted the pragmatist ideas of Charles Sanders Peirce and John Dewey in his design of the Community of Philosophical Inquiry (CPI), a dialogic method intended to foster multidimensional thought (or combined critical, creative, and caring thinking), which he viewed as "a balance between the cognitive and the affective, between the perceptual and the conceptual, between the physical and the mental." (p. 200–201) To this end, a CPI invites its youth participants to share in a philosophical stimulus (like a story, artwork, or aesthetic experiment), formulate questions for conceptual exploration that they deem contestable and central to their lives, and refine their perspectives through structured group dialogue, all the while guided by an adult facilitator who helps to raise their awareness of their evolving thought processes.

Lipman envisioned the CPI method as a collaborative thinking practice with the potential to instil in its members a spirit of self-correction characterized by open-mindedness, epistemological humility, acceptance of fallibility, comfort with uncertainty, resistance to bias, and mutual support—a multi-layered metacognitive disposition aiming toward enhanced awareness of thought processes. Yet although the work involved appears largely intellectual in character, a CPI is also a powerful phenomenological engagement: children sit together in close proximity, encounter each other's lived experiences and sources of meaning, and connect with one another's tone of voice, facial expressions, gestural style, and overall bodily energy. This embodied thinking reflects an aesthetic experience that is palpable and significant, yet often unexplored. As practitioners of this now international, UNESCO-endorsed method, we have been privy to the transformative epiphanies that youth have gained from the multifaceted aesthetic experiences of having their voice taken seriously. Yet we have also sought ways of extending the process through further responses (the last and often neglected CPI stage),[2] not only through meaningful creative projects but also through experimentation that gauges their phenomenological experiences of philosophizing.

The notion of a philosogram emerged from these efforts, and more specifically from a 1-year empirical research study that sought to explore children's reflections on how they experience the process of engaging both in philosophical dialogue through the CPI pedagogical method and in the creative projects that culminate from these collaborative dialogue sessions.[3] The research focused specifically on children's experiences of meaning-making with each other, notably how they make use of their imagination, first to expand the scope of the reasoning they provide in support of their various philosophical positions, and then to extend these positions through creative expression in the form of written works, drawings and photos, visual art, performance, and multimedia. The context for the research project was a series of youth programs offered by Brila, a registered Canadian educational charity that is an affiliate centre of the Institute for the Advancement of Philosophy for Children founded by Lipman.[4] The children participating in the study were members of the charity's youth board, aged 6–16, both anglophone and francophone, who met semi-regularly throughout the school year on weekends and during holidays for workshops and week-long camps. Criteria for inclusion were: first, having experience engaging in CPI practices—that is, knowing how philosophical dialogue operates in informal contexts such as ours—and second, having at least completed kindergarten but not yet graduated high school.

As part of the research, participants were involved in three types of activities.[5] First, they were asked to engage in CPI dialogues as they had grown accustomed to doing during past Brila programs. These CPI dialogues involved them sitting in a circle with 6–10 other children, and collaboratively inquiring on a series of philosophical questions relating to a particular theme of interest, such as: "Can we understand another person's fear?" "Can we imagine something that does not exist?" "Can anyone make art?" "Can images tell a lie?" "Can we tell a story without knowing it?" "Can we communicate without talking?" etc. They took turns sharing their positions, indicating agreement or disagreement, providing examples and counter-examples, offering definitions and distinctions, imagining the consequences of their positions, and improving them in light of their collective idea development. Second, they were invited to produce creative works relating to the philosophical questions and positions they explored through their CPI dialogues, including individual and team projects involving varied artistic media. When necessary, they were asked to explain their creative works, and connect these to the philosophical themes explored. Third, at the end of the study, they participated in semi-structured, face-to-face interviews in small groups, inspired by applied phenomenological research methods, to reflect on their experiences of engaging in CPI-style philosophical dialogues and associated creative expression. The interview questions were not pre-determined but emerged and evolved based on the groups' responses and reflections in relation to certain relevant themes, after which point they created their own philosograms in an effort to capture the phenomenological dimensions of their philosophical experimentation—itself a powerful aesthetic experience.

DISTINCTIVE AESTHETIC EXPERIENCES

Our initial experiment with philosograms has prompted us to wonder: How is an encounter with artwork different from engagement in philosophical dialogue? White has argued that aesthetic experience is a multifaceted, individualized occurrence that progresses from multi-sensory perception at the physical level to a state of awareness connecting to related or universal experiences at the spiritual level, and finally to a sense of personal significance at the mental level, and as such "involves the whole person—body, mind, and spirit."[6] Based on this description, it is easy to see the similarities between an encounter with artwork and an engagement with CPI-style philosophy since both are holistic in like ways: they constitute a powerful, potentially transformative process that is embodied and affectively charged, while also enabling meaning-making that can feel transcendent in its capacity to illuminate thinking and help frame the world differently. Lipman (2003) himself described collaborative philosophical inquiry as a kind of aesthetic encounter since "a mental act is an achievement, a performance. One can feel oneself moving toward the making of a decision and then making it ... A mental act is therefore like a tiny work of art." (p. 143) So it seems possible that the analysis of such mental acts in a philosogram—like the analysis of an artwork in an aesthetigram—can yield similar benefits.

However, there are also important differences between aesthetic experiences in art and in philosophy. As explored throughout this book, an aesthetigram captures individuals' aesthetic experiences of a singular artwork, and even their re-engagement with it over time and after other types of exposure. They are tasked with immersing themselves in an artwork, then mapping out their global experience using specific criteria that hone in on both their observations of specific, formal aspects of the art as well as their reflections on their own wide-ranging personal responses to it in light of their lived experiences and knowledge. In contrast, a philosogram intends to map out individuals' overall aesthetic experiences of engaging in collaborative philosophical inquiry as an evolving practice to which they have already committed a significant amount of time and energy. This means focusing not on one singular dialogue (as aesthetigrams focus on one single artwork at a time), but rather analysing multiple dialogues with others across a substantial period of regular meetings. Further, unlike aesthetigrams, which represent one person's dynamic immersion with an artwork, the object of analysis in a philosogram is not an individualized process but necessarily a collective one, adding many layers of interpretation: How did others' perspectives affect the elaboration of my own? How did I influence them? How did group dynamics contribute to my thinking and meaning-making? As such, the phenomenological modes represented by the categories in a philosogram are designed to represent an individual's experience, but that very experience is embedded in a complex intersubjective process. Though the categories are in no way fixed, some current ones include:

questioning: "you wonder about the topic and ask for clarification"
imagining: "you visualize or dream up scenarios and possibilities"
feeling: "you have emotions about the topic, the dialogue and the process"
knowing: "you share your knowledge or facts about the topic"
storytelling: "you share a memory or experience"
judging: "you form a position on the topic or question"
connecting: "you build on someone else's idea or find links between your own"
doubting: "you are unsure or confused about your ideas or others' ideas"
sensing: "you react with your body and senses"

The aim of these categories is to probe the question: What is it like doing philosophy with others in this dialogical mode? For children, we put the question another way to get them describing their insider experience as if to an outsider audience: How would they describe their philosophy dialogues to an alien who knew nothing about them? Given its interpretive load and the abstract self-assessments involved, this mapping process could seem daunting, especially for elementary school children. Yet thanks to our closeness with the participants—our strong bonds after many hours of collaborative work and play over time—they were more than willing to try their hand at philosograms. It is important to note that in all cases, Brila programs have been the participants' only experience of philosophy, so when they hear the term, it denotes not only the CPI-style dialogue that Brila uses but also the charity's specific take on it, which has become a part of their growing up and informal education. This reality changes the nature of philosophy for the purpose of this discussion: As we decided as a group, "We're calling it philosophy because we're asking big questions, we're thinking about the answers and we're sharing our ideas."[7]

A PHILOSOGRAM IN CONTEXT

So what might a philosogram look like in context? For the purposes of illustration, we will consider the philosogram experiment of one child, a nine-year old third-grader we will call Logan. At the start of his interview, when asked what is it like doing philosophy, Logan's description reveals his enthusiasm for the CPI model and his evolving metacognitive capacities:

Well you're asking a question about questioning! We're in a philosophy circle and you're asking us about the philosophy circle. I think about thinking about thinking about thinking. It's very satisfying! How I would describe it is: It's basically a circle where you ask questions and we say what we think about them, and we give our opinion, and if people disagree, they'll say what they think, and at the end, we end up with a conclusion. You discuss things and you change maybe how you think and your point of view … you're actually thinking about things that other people wouldn't necessarily think of. Like, would you sacrifice one person to save a whole group? And then we ask questions about our questions and all of that! I would describe it as plain fun.

Since we wanted to have a sense of how participants felt about the collaborative nature of the CPI model, we invited them to share their impressions of engaging in philosophizing with others, and were surprised by their enthusiasm toward this admittedly challenging process, with Logan's response being no exception:

> I think being with more people, it gives you more information and it makes you think of a lot of different things, more than just being alone. When other people disagree with you and you're trying to think of something and your own opinion, and mix it up with what they think to make a conclusion, it's hard because there's a lot of things to think about. You don't really know if they're right or wrong, so you don't know what to believe. But I consider what they're saying and take it in my mind. I wouldn't just stay on my idea. I'd see if their idea in a way is better. So everybody gives their ideas—it's better to have more people!

Lastly, bearing in mind our specific interest in the participants' phenomenological experiences, we asked them to describe how it feels in their body to do philosophy, and Logan asked if he could offer what he thought was an amusing but apt analogy:

> So I would say judging on right now that how I feel is kind of weird. How I feel is like a sausage cooking on the BBQ. For me, when I look at the sausage, there is the juice coming out, and it gives me the feeling of tension and I don't know why. Just like in the philosophy circles, there's so much information; it's fun talking and all of that, but it feels like it's a lot, a lot, a lot. And you're getting a lot of information out of my head and I have to work hard to go deep, deep, deep into my brain to get the answers that I think of.

Interestingly, when came the time to create his philosogram, Logan's mapping clearly reflected his notion of "mixing up" his ideas with others, and expressed his experiences of tension from tough concentrated work, which is in line with our impression of him as a highly collaborative, perseverant yet playful thinker. Logan was asked to map out the stages he goes through in his experiences of thinking in a CPI, using differently sized, colour-coded, and connected circles (much like in an aesthetigram) to represent the intensities of his various phenomenological "moments." We helped to scaffold this process since, though the research participants were used to "going meta" at Brila programs by metacognitively analysing their thinking during dialogues with visual and tactile aids, and afterwards in group assessments, this kind of diagramming—especially of the more tacit and ineffable components—was less familiar.

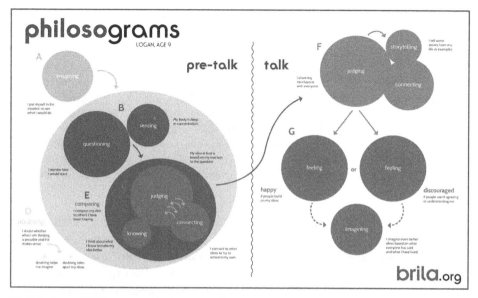

Fig 7.1. Logan's Philosogram (Author created).

As a whole, Logan's philosogram stands out as having a clearly delineated "thinking zone" and "talking zone"—he does a lot of sorting out in his head before he feels ready to share his ideas with the group.[8] At first, his "imagining" moment takes precedence to orient him to the philosophical question at hand and toward a possible response: "I start by imagining myself in that situation and what I would do personally then I kind of build up on what I would do. And then after I imagine it, I see what I can improve about my idea." From then on, his pre-talk moments are englobed in an all-encompassing feeling of doubt that he experiences as both positive and negative at the corporeal and affective levels:

> I'm questioning myself. I question myself about how I would react and how it has a connection to other things. My body is very concentrated. I doubt myself to see if maybe I went too far or something. I ask myself before I say it—if it's possible, if it makes sense. I doubt myself at each stage. But only after the imagining stage because I can't doubt myself on nothing! [Laughs] I'm doubting if for example [my idea] is possible, because I don't want to say something that's impossible, like unicorns flying because I don't think unicorns exist personally. I'm trying to figure out if my idea is actually good or not.

On his view, Logan's doubting feels negative in the sense that he is downplaying and taking out parts of what he originally thought through self-critique but also positive in the sense that it helps to push his imagination forward in generating stronger ideas. Once Logan has gone through this stage, he feels primed to move from what he calls the "thinking zone" in his brain to the "talking zone" with the group. He depicts his own ideas as a half-circle in need of completion by other people's contributions, while noting the fine line between thinking with others and thinking for himself. He describes this process as a "mixing up" or "blobbing together":

> After I raise my hand to talk and then after I say my ideas, and after other people talk, then I try to improve my idea with what other people are saying. That's what I mean about mixing it up. So there's a blob of what others say and a blob of what I say, and it connects. It goes back and forth until it's smushed together. I mix it up with what other people say to make a conclusion that everyone would agree with. Getting inspired by other people. Taking my idea but not completely reinventing what I would say. Because that would be like copying other people!

For Logan, his "talking zone" also tends to include a storytelling moment that guards against his concern for copying others. So when he shares his idea with the group, he is also concretizing it with examples—drawing from "what I know from all kinds of stuff, from stories, from living what I live." This experience of sharing his ideas with others elicits different feeling moments, depending on the reactions he garners from the group: "I feel happy when people build on my ideas and agree with them. I feel kind of discouraged when people don't agree, but at the same time I feel like I should build on what they are disagreeing on and come up with a conclusion." Of note, for Logan, the collaborative aspect of the dialogue enables his good and bad feelings to "blob together" with the ideas themselves, which in turn makes him feel more productive and successful at answering the given philosophical question: "It's two paths that can lead to the same thing. It makes me imagine—imagine another thinking. Out of all the thinking, I kind of combine it with a feeling and make it better." On the whole, Logan worked through the stages of his thinking experience with relative ease and admirable openness. When he decided his philosogram was complete, we asked him if he thought it represented his process, and he responded with the witty candour we have come to expect of him: "Yeah! But I think my brain is maybe a bit messier. Maybe … I've never actually seen my brain!"

CHALLENGES WITH PHILOSOGRAMS

While this first experiment of facilitating children's philosograms was satisfying and inspiring in many ways—not least in the participants' ease with and enjoyment of the process—even at this preliminary research stage, we have already noted key challenges, notably those of generalization and self-awareness. First, our very choice to focus on mapping a generalized experience of collaborative philosophical inquiry may be inherently problematic. Is it indeed the case that individuals engaged in a CPI practice have certain consistent experiences worth noting? Do they undergo similar phenomenological moments across these multiple engagements, or do these depend on outside factors, like the chosen inquiry question, the group's constitution, the mood of day? Would it be more advisable to do a philosogram for each dialogue (as an aesthetigram focuses on one artwork), or even one for the group as a whole, or are there significant patterns over time that make this kind of individual aesthetic experience distinct from those involved in art encounters? In short, can this kind of aesthetic experience really be generalized?

From our preliminary data, the participants' responses suggest there may indeed be significant patterns worth attending to in order to better understand children's experience of philosophizing—for example, the time it takes Logan to warm to a question through a process of imagining, doubting, and questioning before he feels equipped to share his thoughts with others. Yet if the philosogram is going to be cumulative in that it represents a series of philosophical encounters taken as one global aesthetic experience, the mapping instructions and options must be flexible enough to illustrate variations depending on external factors and personal growth in the thinking practice. For instance, one participant chose not to label her moments with sequential letters, opting against a linear model in favour of a philosogram with multiple entry points to show how she gets from thinking to talking regardless of the question being explored, the attitudes of the group or her own frame of mind at any particular meeting. This need for flexibility might require the creation of many more possible categories that capture other phenomenological dimensions of the experience that we have not yet addressed. Conversely, it may involve having no categories at all to begin, and instead starting off with the children's own descriptions of their experiences that they then label as they see fit, thereby avoiding the possibly restrictive or steering character of pre-set categories. In attempting the philosogram mapping during a separate exploratory workshop, some of our adult colleagues suggested that a legend of different arrows and lines between moments could be helpful to indicate connections that do or do not happen depending on aspects specific to the dialogues themselves—for example, a dotted line to express a feeling moment that tends to happen only if one's idea is not taken up by the group. Such nuances might help to address the challenge of generalizing multiple and potentially incongruent engagements of CPI-style philosophy into one aesthetic experience, which may in turn result in philosograms with more interpretive integrity.

A second challenge involves the level of self-awareness required to create a philosogram, including the capacities for memory, metacognitive focus, and honesty. First, in terms of memory, if participants are required to think back to their experiences of collaborative philosophical inquiry over time, they will have to rely on recollections of dialogues that may have occurred months prior to their mapping, making their representations more fallible and leaving them at the mercy of their powers of retention. They will also have to make a concerted effort at every engagement to remain as self-aware as possible in terms of their phenomenological experiences in order to have memories that will be eventually useful to their mapping. As Fróis and White (2013) have noted, in this kind of diagramming, we are "reliant upon records of the layered and linked moments of the individual participants' experiences." (p. 110) Second, in terms of metacognitive focus, during CPI dialogues, since participants are not singlehandedly in control of the process but rather sharing control of it with their co-inquirers, the experience may seem harder to capture in philosogram form compared to a personal aesthetic experience of a singular artwork in an aesthetigram. Can they think about their individual and collective thinking, and actively wonder about how others are thinking—or is this too demanding of children who are already attempting the difficult task of coming up with reasonable philosophical positions together? Can they be expected to map out their phenomenological experiences of a practice they are still grappling to understand, equipped with crucial but still budding metacognitive capacities? Third, the process of a philosogram seems to necessarily involve a self-evaluative component—participants are invited not only to analyse their experience but also to sincerely appraise who they are in that experience, both the good and the bad, their strengths and their limitations. This requires an extreme form of honesty that might be easy to accidentally or purposefully avoid: participants could likely create a philosogram illustrating how they hope they are in their philosophical dialogues with others rather than how they actually are. In other words, they may idealize their aesthetic experience. For example, one participant realized with some hesitancy and shame that during CPI dialogues, he initially has a moment of "knowing" that can overshadow and even trivialize others' contributions, a tendency he is not proud of and wants to change. While such realizations represent meaningful learning moments, we cannot assume that all participants will be willing or able to offer the same honest self-appraisals.

OPPORTUNITIES WITH PHILOSOGRAMS

While the challenges of generalization and self-awareness cannot be discounted, and we ought certainly to investigate and address other problematic components of philosograms, we do see opportunities that are too important to dismiss, especially in terms of self-correction and enhanced intersubjective understanding. First, the potential of philosograms to help support self-corrective dispositions is worth examining. As already mentioned, while there may be a tendency in children (and for that matter, adults) to idealize their philosograms for fear of appearing less competent or cooperative, the habits of honest self-appraisal that could be cultivated with the right pedagogical framing are crucial. Arguably, the way philosograms are introduced as an educational activity would have to emphasize the all-important role of self-correction that the CPI model espouses, highlighting how the mapping process may unearth difficulties and weaknesses that participants currently exhibit as individuals or as a group. By extension, to make philosograms effective as an educational tool for enhancing self-awareness and motivating self-improvement, we may have to ask children to recreate them at key intervals to see if certain tendencies have evolved or devolved, then provide opportunities for them to devise strategies to address ongoing issues. Put differently, philosograms seem able to act as mirrors of individual and collective growth in a CPI practice, and to that end, they may have to be adapted to help support children's philosophical progress. In the same way that aesthetigrams foster practices of looking, seeing, and interpreting, philosograms may be in a position to cultivate the practice of being thoughtful, understood in both senses: as being "deeply absorbed in thought and characterized by careful reasoning—reflective, mindful, discerning"; and "showing genuine consideration for others and concern of their treatment— attentive, empathetic, big-hearted."9

In a sense, even if children's philosograms are "wrong" in that they are not exact representations of their thinking practice, they are still useful as an exercise that seeks to attune them to their phenomenological experiences of philosophizing with others.

This self-corrective potential highlights a second key opportunity that philosograms appear to enable, namely enhanced intersubjective understanding, both among children and between children and adults. One anecdotal observation that struck us about our initial experimentation with philosograms is how strongly they resonated with our own experience of the participants as CPI members—we recognized the children in their diagrams and agreed with the mapping of their thinking stages, enabling a kind of intimacy with who they are as emerging philosophers. At the same time, their philosograms helped us better understand how they perceived the meaning of their various idiosyncrasies as inquirers, both at the level of their bodies and their self-talk. One of our six-year-old participants explained why she often finds herself curled up into a tight cross-legged position, holding her feet and oscillating:

> It's like a clock going, 'Tick-tock, the time will run out, quick hurry up!' And the movement shakes up my ideas, and my answers are all turning around, and when I stop, an answer is in the middle of my head and I decide if it's a good one. If it is, I say it; if it's not, I keep swinging.

She confirms this hurried feeling is self-imposed because she does not want the session to end without her sharing her thoughts. When she finally does, she feels "timid but at the same time proud of myself—I don't know if my idea is brilliant but I know that I made an effort." This kind of privileged access into our participants' phenomenological experience of philosophizing has been especially helpful with our neurodiverse populations. One such participant in second grade used the metaphor of a volcano in his philosogram to explain how his body feels during philosophical inquiry:

> I sometimes feel so excited that when you ask the question, I wonder to myself and it takes a few seconds, and then it's the volcano that explodes! If I'm tired, the ideas wake me up. I am excited by my answer and I put up my hand right away! But I still don't know if what I am giving can help others understand me ...

Such descriptions have made it easier for us as facilitators to interpret his outbursts of enthusiasm and his occasional reluctance to connect with others' perspectives, while providing the figurative language to help him establish strategies that he is comfortable trying out—he now tells us when his volcano is nearing eruption and he needs a break because he is having trouble paying attention to the group.

Further, the visual depictions of each participant's phenomenological moments when they philosophize has acted as a kind of invitation to other children to better understand and appreciate how they each experience their collective dialogues differently or similarly, heightening the possibilities for empathy and attentive listening. After all, it seems reasonable to assume that if children are more attuned to how their co-inquirers engage in collaborative philosophy, they may be more likely to be patient, constructive, unprejudiced, and supportive when things go awry or when their feeling moments become too intense. For instance, one participant noted that she personally needed to come up with an answer to a given question right away in order to feel any kind of progress. But in realizing that her friend had almost the opposite need—to tentatively explore and diverge before hypothesizing—she could acknowledge how everyone seemed to work through these difficult questions in their own unique (though still comparable) ways. Accordingly, philosograms could be in a position to help children see how others are valuable in ways they are not, allowing them to further recognize the importance of CPI-style philosophy's intersubjective dimensions. Given this possibility, it would be worth further exploring through empirical research how the metacognitive process of creating philosograms affects future participation in a CPI and even extends to conduct in other contexts.

CONCLUSION

The CPI method featured in this study was originally developed in no small part to help give children a voice and demonstrate their capacity to engage in complex philosophical thinking from a young age. It is our hope that the research findings from philosograms will eventually contribute to this demonstration, by showcasing children not only engaged in philosophical dialogue and associated creative projects but also in metacognitive reflection on their phenomenological experiences of such experimentation in light of their current lived experiences. According to the adolescent participants in our study, philosograms are an important process because through them, children can attempt to make sense of an experience that they do not often have in their lives, particularly not at school. In the words of one of our 16 year olds: "This place of philosophy is very different. We're trying to find something that is universal to everyone in all concepts. In some situations where you find yourself trying to make a decision and trying to know what's right and what's wrong, and what you should do, it's only based on what you know, what you have gone through and what has been taught to you. But you don't have other minds with you, speaking what they think from their experience." With more fine-tuning and participant feedback, we hope the philosogram approach can enable those interested in collaborative philosophical inquiry, especially young people, to explore their experiences of philosophizing with others to capture, among other dimensions, that distinctive feeling of "having other minds with them."

NOTES

1. The idea of philosograms came from earlier experience with aesthetigrams as part of Dr. White's research—a philosophical adaptation seemed like a possible outgrowth of that initial experience.
2. Lipman designed the CPI method as a five-stage dialogical inquiry process involving a group of youth and a trained P4C facilitator. As originally conceived, the stages proceed as follows: "Stage 1. The offering of the text: Students read or enact a philosophical story together; Stage 2. The construction of the agenda: Students raise questions for discussion and organize them into an agenda; Stage 3. Solidifying the community: Students discuss questions as a community of inquiry facilitated by an adult with philosophical training; Stage 4. Using exercises and discussion plans: The philosophical facilitator introduces relevant activities to deepen and expand the students' inquiry; Stage 5. Encouraging further responses: These include self-assessment of philosophy practice, art projects and action projects." In Maughn Gregory, "Normative Dialogue Types in Philosophy for Children," Gifted Education International, 2007, 22(1): 163.
3. This study, entitled "Making Meaning Together: Children's Reflections on their Experiences of Philosophical Dialogue and Creative Projects," was conducted with the approval of Concordia University's Research Ethics Unit and received its Certification of Ethical Acceptability for Research Involving Human Subjects (30005538) on January 25, 2016.
4. Brila is a registered charity under the Canada Revenue Agency (#82689 1251 RR0001) and a nationally incorporated non-for-profit under Industry Canada (#544102). For information: www.brila.org
5. Information for the research project was gathered from various sources: data from professional practice and programs run through Brila, data from semi-structured face-to-face audio-recorded interviews of youth participants, and data from youth participants' audio-recorded philosophical

dialogues and creative projects (e.g., stories, poems, illustrations, photography, visual artworks, performance, and multimedia works). The information provided never had identifiers associated with it, and the data has since been pseudonymized to protect the identity of participants.

6. From the Introduction in this text. See page xiv.
7. This and all following excerpts come from transcripts of audio recorded dialogues as part of the empirical study "Making Meaning Together: Children's Reflections on their Experiences of Philosophical Dialogue and Creative Projects" (2016).
8. Please see the digital reproduction of Logan's philosogram on page.
9. This take on thoughtfulness comes from Brila's educational philosophy: as a youth-driven charity, Brila strives to help young people practice being reasonable and imaginative together, while developing the sensibility necessary to decide what is worth discussing, expressing, and pursuing: www.brila.org/workshops.

REFERENCES

Fróis, J. P. & White, B. (2013). Words for Artworks: The Aesthetics of Meaning Making. *The International Journal of Art & Design Education, 32*(1), 109–125.

Gregory, M. (2007). Normative Dialogue Types in Philosophy for Children. *Gifted Education International, 22*(1), 160–171.

Lipman, M. (2003). *Thinking in Education*. Cambridge, MA: Cambridge University Press.

RELATED READINGS

Gregory, M., Haynes, J. & Murris, K. (Eds.) (2016). *The Routledge International Handbook of Philosophy for Children*. New York: Routledge.

Gregory, M. (2006). Pragmatist Value Inquiry. *Contemporary Pragmatism, 3*(1), 107–128.

Haynes, J. & Murris, K. (2012). *Picturebooks, Pedagogy and Philosophy*. New York: Routledge.

Kennedy, D. (2010). *Philosophical Dialogue with Children: Essays on Theory and Practice*. Lewiston, New York: The Edwin Mellen Press, 2010.

Kennedy, D. (2006). *The Well of Being: Childhood, Subjectivity, and Education*. Albany: SUNY Press.

Lipman, M. & Sharp, A. (Eds.) (1994). *Growing Up with Philosophy*. Dubuque, IA: Kendall-Hunt.

Lipman, M. (1998). *Philosophy Goes to School*. Philadelphia: Temple University Press.

Lipman, M., Sharp, A. M. & Oscanyan, F. S. (1980). *Philosophy in the Classroom* (2nd ed). Philadelphia, PA: Temple University Press, 1980.

Sharp, A. (1997). The Aesthetic Dimension of the Community of Inquiry. *Inquiry: Critical Thinking Across the Disciplines, 17*(1), 67–77.

Contributor's Bio

Chapter 7, Natalie M. Fletcher is founding director of Brila Youth Projects in Montreal (www.brila.org), an educational charity that fosters children's multi-dimensional thinking through philosophical dialogue and creative projects. Her research fuses the fields of ethics, political philosophy, dialogic pedagogy and aesthetics education.

Index

Figures in this index are indicated by an italicized page number.